HAM'

AS AND A-LEV

GUID

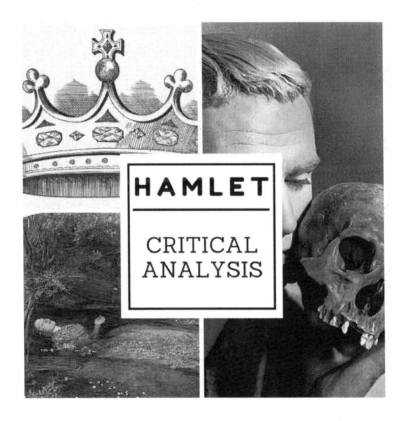

HAMLET

**CRITICAL
ANALYSIS**

CHARLOTTE UNSWORTH

CONTENTS

WHAT TO EXPECT FROM THIS GUIDE

This is aimed at the OCR specification in particular and so assessment objectives etc relate to that specification. However, there's plenty which will be relevant to A-Level students.

There's a LOT of Hamlet revision guides out there. My aim for this one is to be as specific as possible for the OCR spec, and in particular to help students get enough knowledge for the play, while bearing in mind that the assessment is closed book. So there is a scene by scene analysis, but in each one I focus on a few key phrases, as well as aspects of form and structure that I think are often easier to learn for this kind of assessment. There is absolutely a place for quotation – but it doesn't have to be as daunting as it might first appear.

In addition, there's also some information on critical viewpoints over time – AO5 – and I've written these to show how to use these selectively, to explore the text in the exam. .

ASSESSMENT OBJECTIVES: WHAT DO THEY MEAN?

AO1:	Articulate informed, personal and creative responses in literary texts, using associated concepts and terminology and coherent, accurate written expression
Can you write an expressive, detailed and well organised essay? Have you got something interesting to say, and can you show that you confidently understand the play? Can you use literary vocabulary confidently, appropriately and selectively? Is your writing always accurate and developed?	
AO2:	Analyse ways in which meanings are shaped in literary texts
How does Shakespeare use language, form and structure to convey his ideas? What specific words, phrases and literary techniques are important in understanding his major themes and ideas? How is stagecraft important in presenting this play?	
AO3:	Demonstrate understanding of the significances and influences of the contexts in which literary texts are written and received
How is Shakespeare affected – consciously or otherwise – by the time in which he lived and wrote? How do his religious, social and political views	

come across in his work? As modern readers, what do we think of his portrayal?	
AO5:	**Explore literary texts informed by different interpretations.**
Can you explore alternative interpretations of the character and theme? Do you understand a range of critical interpretations – sometimes a theory (e.g. feminism, Marxism), and sometimes a specific critic? Can you explore a range of interpretations across time?	

ANALYSIS OF THE PLAY

Notes on analysis:

Because the exam is closed book, it's important to have a range of quotations. There's a later section about how to write about form and structure to meet the AO2 requirements, and I've written more about that on my blog as well, but throughout this analysis I've suggested some key quotations as a starting point. I've also underlined key sections in longer quotes, so that the longer context remains visible, but the underlined section would be a useful part to memorise. Also see the later section on how to select quotes to remember.

You *may* find that some lines here are slightly different to the version you have. I've used the Shakespeare Online text – but because of the different copies of *Hamlet* that we have (see Context) there are slight variations. Use the version that you have, and adapt any notes as needed – these minor differences are fine, and won't count against you in an exam whichever you use.

ACT I SCENE I

PLOT SUMMARY:

The scene opens at Elsinore castle in Denmark. On the ramparts, the guards Barnardo and Francisco are keeping watch. Marcellus and Horatio come to meet them - and to see if their story about seeing the ghost of the old King Hamlet is true. Horatio is sceptical, but they assure him it is real. They've asked Horatio partly because he's friends with the young Hamlet, Prince of Denmark, and because he's a scholar – the belief was that only the educated could speak to the dead.

The ghost refuses to speak but, recognising the ghost as the old King, Horatio talks about the war in which he died. The audience learns that Denmark and Norway have been warring, and the old King Hamlet slew their king, Fortinbras. Just to confuse matters, both their sons were also called Hamlet and Fortinbras – and the young Fortinbras has taken his father's death hard, and sworn revenge.

Horatio and Marcellus discuss whether the ghost is holy or not, and resolve to tell his son Hamlet of its presence.

KEY THEMES:

Religion – the afterlife, and what happens to us. Is the old Hamlet doomed to haunt the castle? Why is he lingering and not in heaven? There's constant conflict over whether the ghost has come from heaven or hell, and it's unclear here.

The reference Marcellus makes to the labourers who "Do not divide the Sunday from the week" implies that the new King, Claudius, has had his men working on the Sabbath – against the commands of religion. It's the first hint that there's something wrong in Denmark now.

The ghost disappears when the cock crows – this is a biblical allusion to the death of Christ (being betrayed before the cock crows), suggesting that the ghost is not heavenly after all.

Sight – Marcellus says Horatio "may approve our eyes" – seeing is believing, after all. After seeing the ghost, Horatio says "I might not this believe/ Without the sensible and true avouch/Of mine own eyes." It's only after seeing the ghost for himself that Horatio can believe their stories.

Honour and masculinity – The old King is described as honourable, "fair" and "warlike" – it's clear what they prize in their masculinity here! Fortinbras is young, untried and foolish in comparison – not a real man at all.

The supernatural – The ghost of the old king is a herald of trouble – the supernatural is by definition **un**natural, and therefore there is something wrong both with his presence and, by extension, with the kingdom.

FORM, STRUCTURE AND LANGUAGE

Opening – the scene starts at night, on the ramparts of Elsinore castle in Denmark. This creates the sense of suspense and intrigue, as well as giving the suitable location for the ghost! We learn about the honour of the old king and, by extension, his young son, in comparison with the difficulties hinted at in Denmark with the ignoring of the commandment not to work on the Sabbath. *See Context for initial performance issues*

Form: The revenge tragedy (see *Context* at the end) often starts with a ghost, who tells the rest of the characters something that starts the story – Shakespeare uses a classic revenge tragedy structure.

CONTEXT:

Renaissance beliefs in the importance of scholars – Horatio may be able to speak to the ghost because he's educated.

Religious beliefs, particularly regarding the ghost, and the conflict between Claudius and other religious attitudes.

KEY QUOTATIONS

Horatio: That fair and warlike form

Describing the old King, Horatio uses "warlike" to impress on the audience the masculinity and nobility of Hamlet – to prime us to believe he was a good king and prepare us for the contrasting approach of Claudius.

Horatio: Young Fortinbras, / Of unimproved mettle hot and full

In contrast, Fortinbras is "hot and full", tempestuous and young, contrastingly unimpressive impetuous and potentially dangerous. However, this contrasts with the description of him at the end, when he is the last man standing, and appears to be highly regal, moral and noble – the rightful successor to the Danish throne.

Marcellus:

It faded on the crowing of the cock.
Some say that ever 'gainst that season comes
Wherein our Saviour's birth is celebrated,
The bird of dawning singeth all night long:
And then, they say, <u>no spirit dares stir abroad</u>;
The nights are wholesome; then no planets strike,
No fairy takes, nor witch hath power to charm,
<u>So hallow'd and so gracious is the time</u>.

The approaching season is Christmas; the time of year is "so hallow'd and gracious" that "no spirit dares stir abroad". The statement implies that the ghost is more holy, despite disappearing when the cock crew, because how else would it be able to walk the earth at such a religious time?

ACT I SCENE 2

PLOT SUMMARY:

The action moves to a room of state in the castle.

In Denmark, succession laws have meant that old Hamlet's brother Claudius has become king – the young Hamlet is next in line *after* him. Claudius gives a speech lamenting his brother's death – but also announcing that he has married Hamlet's widow, Gertrude, and expects everyone to be happy about it!

Claudius then turns not to Hamlet as might be expected, but to Laertes, son of Polonius (an advisor to the king). Laertes returned from studying for the King's funeral and the following wedding, and begs leave to return – which is granted, and Claudius tells Laertes how grateful the crown is to him for his loyalty.

Claudius and Gertrude then turn to Hamlet, and ask him to be more cheerful, to stop wearing his mourning clothes for his father and instead celebrate their marriage. Claudius tells him that continuing to mourn is insulting and childish while Gertrude asks him to be happier. They also ask him to remain in Denmark rather than return to Wittenberg, where he was studying before his father's death.

When they leave the stage and Hamlet is left alone, Hamlet utters his first soliloquy – a mournful rant against the unfairness of his father's death and the hasty nature of his mother's marriage – it's one of many times when he seems more angered by the marriage than the death.

Horatio and Marcellus come to find him, and tell him that they have seen his father's ghost – he agrees to watch with them the next night to see for himself.

KEY THEMES:

Love – Are Claudius and Gertrude in love? At some points in the play it seems as though they are – see *Critical Interpretations* for further discussion of Gertrude's role.

Honour and duty: Claudius tells Hamlet that to mourn his father is honourable – but only to a point. Then, he has a duty to the living around him, to Denmark, even to God, to cease mourning

Women and sexuality: Hamlet is often angrier with Gertrude's re-marrying than over the fact of his father's death. His soliloquy (see below) is often more concerned with her apparent sexual misconduct and the betrayal he feels at the short time she has spent mourning.

FORM, STRUCTURE AND LANGUAGE

Claudius' speech to the court – See below for close analysis. The king's speech here is an incredibly important one – it's the first he's giving to the court in his new position as King, and revealing to them his marriage to his sister-in-law. He speaks in blank verse and uses a series of parallelisms and closely linked images to highlight his suggestion that he is the best option for Denmark, that his succession and the wedding are natural occurrences.

Moving from outside to inside moves the focus from the supernatural and the natural laws of good and evil to politics, and man-made laws of the same. Outside, the conflict is whether the ghost is good or evil; inside, the conflict is over Claudius' motivations.

Impressions of Claudius and Hamlet: always remember that this is designed to be seen, and not studied! So, in this case, consider the initial impressions of the family unit we're presented with. Claudius, despite turning first to Laertes, is kind, conciliatory, measured and apparently caring. But Hamlet is moody, difficult and deliberately goads his uncle.

Turning first to Laertes however, tells us that Claudius is possible more concerned with politics than family.

The scene ends with Hamlet alone, and a rhyming couplet:

Hamlet: My father's spirit in arms! all is not well;
I doubt some foul play: would the night were come!
Till then sit still, my soul: foul deeds will rise,
Though all the earth o'erwhelm them, to men's eyes.

Rhyming couplets often increase the sense of finality and summarise the emotional impact of a scene – here the final message of the scene is that evil will always be found out, and this is a great statement to really kick off the action. It implies to the audience that the ghost is here, typical of a revenge tragedy, to reveal something terrible and that the rest of the play will be about the discovery of this evil deed and its impact on the characters. It's also a great line to summarise the rest of the play – the idea that fate will always ensure that "foul deeds" will be discovered, so the audience is always waiting to discover how this occurs.

11

CONTEXT:

The succession question

Roles and expectations of women – Hamlet's angrier with Gertrude for marrying, than that his father is dead.

KEY QUOTATIONS

Hamlet: Seems, madam! nay it is; I know not 'seems.'

Hamlet's anger is at the suggestion that he is feigning mourning; or at least feigning more than he genuinely feels. He argues, through a series of negatives, that he feels just as he presents himself – others "might play" but he genuinely feels this unhappy;

Claudius:
'tis unmanly grief;
It shows a will most incorrect to heaven,
A heart unfortified, a mind impatient,
An understanding simple and unschool'd
A direct criticism of Hamlet, and an indication of what "masculinity" should be – Hamlet is too weak, because he is grieving too much. The question of Hamlet's madness is important too, as it's often considered in Elizabethan times to be an indicator of a weak mind, of low intellect – so here, Hamlet is susceptible to it. By referring to the "heart" and the "mind" Claudius links them both, suggesting Hamlet is too emotional. And mot rational enough.

Hamlet: I shall in all my best obey you, madam.

When asked to stay in Denmark rather than go back to university, Hamlet clearly says he will obey "You" – his mother – rather than his uncle and king. An insult to Claudius, whom he despises, but also significant that here at least Hamlet shows some respect to Gertrude.

Hamlet: Thrift, thrift, Horatio! the funeral baked meats / Did coldly furnish forth the marriage tables.

Useful for discussing the haste of the marriage – the idea that the two ceremonies followed so swiftly that the leftovers of one could be used for the other. The reference to speed is one of the criticisms levelled at Gertrude, implying that her haste is unseemly, and raising questions about her sexual desires being the driving force behind her remarriage.

Horatio: A countenance more in sorrow than in anger.

CLOSE ANALYSIS:

Claudius' first address to the court

Though yet of Hamlet our dear brother's death
The memory be green, and that it us befitted
To bear our hearts in grief and our whole kingdom
To be contracted in one brow of woe,
Yet so far hath discretion fought with nature
That we with wisest sorrow think on him,
Together with remembrance of ourselves.

Using the royal plural "we" and "our" reminds the court that Claudius is now king, and emphasises his authority. By linking the "green" memory with "nature", he also tells them that he believes that moving on is as natural as grieving. The whole monologue is delivered in blank verse, which creates a measured, musical feeling; the lyricism and stately nature of this speech oozes authority, and to the watching court – and audience – creates an impression of Claudius as thoughtful and regal: the natural king. The semantic field of mourning – "grief", "woe", "sorrow" – all tell us how unhappy he is at the death of his brother – but how much of this is true, and how much is for show? The conflict he describes as "discretion fought with nature" is just one of a series of contradictions in his speech.

Therefore our sometime sister, now our queen,
The imperial jointress to this warlike state,
Have we, as 'twere with a defeated joy,-
With an auspicious and a dropping eye,
With mirth in funeral and with dirge in marriage,
In equal scale weighing delight and dole,--
Taken to wife: nor have we herein barr'd
Your better wisdoms, which have freely gone
With this affair along. For all, our thanks.

The announcement of the marriage is swift, and comes with a series of contradictions – the "mirth in funeral and dirge in marriage", "delight and dole" implying the balanced nature of Claudius' decision; he's had to struggle with the natural desire to grieve, and the need for the royal marriage to take place, owing stability to the kingdom. Considering the succession of Elizabeth I was in question as she had no children and remained unmarried, is this Shakespeare defending his queen – the implication being that Claudius, the villain of the play, has behaved in this unseemly manner but Elizabeth's decision was the right one? It's also perhaps less deliberate on Claudius' part, because it gives an impression of indecision which conflicts with the regal nature of the metre. The caesura "Taken to wife:" creates a pause and directors must decide how much: does Claudius challenge his court there, or quickly rush to the next line to brook no opposition? It depends how authoritative and calculating Claudius is. References to Gertrude don't speak of love or harmony – she's his partner in ruling the kingdom but we're not yet certain what their relationship is like. The end-stopped "For all, our thanks" is a decisive finishing note, the personal business being concluded before he moves onto the more public and political discussion of Fortinbras' approach.

Hamlet's "Too Solid Flesh" soliloquy

O, that this too too solid flesh would melt
Thaw and resolve itself into a dew!
Or that the Everlasting had not fix'd
His canon 'gainst self-slaughter! O God! God!

Hamlet's first soliloquy is delivered alone onstage after the court has left – he's been publicly humiliated by Claudius's disregard, instructed to stay when he wants to leave, and is grieving for his father. The exclamation expresses his anger, and grief, echoed in the fourth line's "Oh God! God!", the repetition emphasising his despair. That God has stated a law against suicide –"self-slaughter" – means Hamlet cannot do it. The religious question of suicide is raised several times in the play – Ophelia, of course, likely committing (unintentional?) suicide in the river later on and her Christian burial questioned by the gravediggers. The "solid" flesh *may* have originally been "sullied", or dirty, soiled. Both spellings suggest that Hamlet sees death for him at this moment as a cleansing, being accepted into heaven

How weary, stale, flat and unprofitable,
Seem to me all the uses of this world!
Fie on't! ah fie! 'tis an unweeded garden,
That grows to seed; things rank and gross in nature
Possess it merely. That it should come to this!

The listing of the state of the world – "weary, stale, flat and unprofitable" exacerbates the impression of Hamlet's misery. There is nothing he would feel the loss of in this world, which makes his relationship with Ophelia suspect later on; how can he, when contemplating suicide here, be genuinely in love with her? Then again, from a modern perspective, we know that isn't truly how mental illness works. Continuing to exclaim his grief, he calls the world an "unweeded garden/that grows to seed", destroyed by the lack of care and attention, and using the metaphor of an Eden neglected and unloved so that only the weeds may flourish there – only the unwanted, or damaging, can survive here. The reference to "things rank and gross in nature" brings his attention back to the initial cause of his despair: his father's death and his mother's marriage.

But two months dead: nay, not so much, not two:
So excellent a king; that was, to this,
Hyperion to a satyr; so loving to my mother
That he might not beteem the winds of heaven
Visit her face too roughly. Heaven and earth!
Must I remember? why, she would hang on him,
As if increase of appetite had grown
By what it fed on: and yet, within a month

Again, the brief interval is stressed - the timeline's tricky (and changes!) so it's possible Hamlet's exaggerating here to dramatise the severity of Gertrude's supposed sin. And again, the old king Hamlet is depicted as being virtually perfect – he's "excellent", like "Hyperion", a sun-god who loved Gertrude so he wouldn't let even the breeze touch her face too roughly, a protector. Yet Claudius is the "satyr", a monstrous creature often used to symbolise a voracious sexual appetite, Hamlet's cry against the curse of memory could be self-pitying, or it could be a genuine cry of grief and betrayal. He recalls the way Gertrude's "appetite had grown", suggesting that she loved him more because she was with him, but also perhaps hinting through the language of food that she is greedy – overly sexualised – and therefore morally dubious.

--
Let me not think on't--Frailty, thy name is woman!--
A little month, or ere those shoes were old
With which she follow'd my poor father's body,
Like Niobe, all tears:--why she, even she--
O, God! a beast, that wants discourse of reason,
Would have mourn'd longer--married with my uncle,
My father's brother, but no more like my father

Than I to Hercules: within a month:
Ere yet the salt of most unrighteous tears
Had left the flushing in her galled eyes,
She married. O, most wicked speed, to post
With such dexterity to incestuous sheets!
It is not nor it cannot come to good:
But break, my heart; for I must hold my tongue.

Towards the middle of his soliloquy Hamlet's language becomes less controlled and deliberate, and although it's still incredibly fragmented the enjambment suggests an angry free-flow of thoughts that he cannot contain. The phrase "frailty, thy name is woman" is crucial in many feminist discussions about the play as this is the turning point at which Gertrude is being explicitly blamed for Hamlet's anger – not his father's death at all. The language emphasises the speed of her decision: the shoes weren't old, her eyes are still "flushing" and red with weeping for King Hamlet as she marries. The reference to Niobe emphasises her sorrow as Niobe is a character from Greek myth associated with weeping following the deaths of her children. The caesura and exclamation – "why she; even she – O God!" – highlights Hamlet's near(but not quite!) speechlessness at her behaviour. Hamlet again criticises Claudius as being "no more like my father/Than I to Hercules". The "dexterity" with which Gertrude goes to her new marriage bed is what condemns her in Hamlet's eyes, her desire to be remarried is a betrayal of his father. The comment about it being "incestuous" is specific to the time-period as the Biblical interpretation of incest includes marrying a brother's wife – downgraded in modern society to adultery. Yet interestingly at the end of **this** soliloquy, Hamlet is going to stay silent – after all, what good would speaking up and criticising do? But of course this is before he knows that his father was murdered.

Watch it!

BBC Poetry by Heart – Watch David Tennant performing this soliloquy:
http://www.bbc.co.uk/schools/teachers/offbyheart/speeches/Hamlet_flesh_would_melt.shtml

ACT I SCENE 3

PLOT SUMMARY:

Laertes and his sister Ophelia say farewell to one another; he warns her to be careful in pursuing a relationship with Hamlet – he's a prince, and she is not a suitable bride for him. She retorts that it's none of his business and, in any case, she could offer him the same advice. However, she does reassure him that he doesn't need to worry.

Polonius, their father, comes to say goodbye as well and gives Laertes some advice, about his financial affairs, friendships, and moral behaviour. When Laertes is gone, he begins to question Ophelia about her relationship with Hamlet. He, too, warns her that Hamlet is above her socially and she should be careful. After a small argument, he commands her to make sure that there is no misunderstanding and she cannot be understood to be having a relationship with Hamlet. She agrees that she will obey his wishes.

KEY THEMES:

Fathers and sons – Polonius' advice to his son is fairly typical of many parents: the difference will be apparent in a later scene, when he sends a spy to ensure Laertes is obeying his advice!

Women and sexuality: Ophelia's honour is questioned by both her brother and father here; although she momentarily fights back, with both of them, ultimately she agrees to make sure that she is above reproach where Hamlet is concerned. Both the men are quite challenging in their language and absolutely appear to have authority over her. She makes a point to Laertes that he should behave as he suggests she should, but her argument with him is nowhere near as confident as some of Shakespeare's other women are, for example Emilia in *Othello*.

FORM, STRUCTURE AND LANGUAGE

Polonius's language of commerce – free, bounteous, tenders – tells Ophelia (and the audience) that her value is measured in what her virginity and honour can provide.

CONTEXT:

Roles and expectations of women

KEY QUOTATIONS

Laertes on Hamlet: his will is not his own;/For he himself is subject to his birth

A warning to Ophelia, but commentary on political reality – monarchs are required to provide an heir. An interesting parallel to Ophelia, who is subject to her father (the kingdom is sometimes referred to here as a fatherland).

Laertes to Ophelia:
Then weigh what loss your honour may sustain,
If with too credent ear you list his songs,
Or lose your heart, or your chaste treasure open
To his unmaster'd importunity.
Fear it, Ophelia, fear it, my dear sister,

Use of language of commerce to suggest the reliance on Ophelia's virginity and honour being unquestionable: she must be beyond reproach. It seems through the list songs, heart, treasure that one thing leads to another, and Ophelia is not safe from gossip if she spends any time with Hamlet. The final endearment may soften the instruction slightly, but Laertes is clearly giving "do as I say" advice, and sees Ophelia as naïve and foolish.

Ophelia:
Do not, as some ungracious pastors do,
Show me the steep and thorny way to heaven;
Whiles, like a puff'd and reckless libertine,
Himself the primrose path of dalliance treads,
And recks not his own rede.

Ophelia rebuffs Laertes – don't give me advice and refuse to follow. A "puff'd and reckless libertine" is harsh criticism indeed. She also contrasts the "steep and thorny way to heaven" with the more comfortable alternative of the "primrose path" – but is she suggesting that perhaps it's not necessarily leading him *away* from heaven?

Ophelia: I do not know, my lord, what I should think.

Polonius to Ophelia:
Marry, well bethought:
'Tis told me, he hath very oft of late
Given private time to you; and you yourself

Have of your audience been most free and bounteous:
If it be so, as so 'tis put on me,
And that in way of caution, I must tell you,
You do not understand yourself so clearly
As it behoves my daughter and your honour.
What is between you? give me up the truth.

Polonius' language of commerce and transaction to describe Ophelia's spending time with Hamlet. The second half here is instructive, the "I must tell you" implying he has no choice, and is compelled – which, as her loving father, he would be, but he is also conscious of the potential damage an unchaste daughter would do to his own reputation. The order of the pronouns "**My** daughter and **your** honour" indicates whose reputation he values most highly. The instruction "give me up the truth" is almost insulting in its assumption that she wouldn't

Polonius:
Marry, I'll teach you: think yourself a baby;
That you have ta'en these tenders for true pay,
Which are not sterling. Tender yourself more dearly;
Or--not to crack the wind of the poor phrase,
Running it thus--you'll tender me a fool.

Ophelia introduced the word "tender" – Hamlet has "made tenders" of his affection, meaning given her letters but also the idea of a tenderness or affection. Polonius plays on this word, to suggest the commercial "tender" linked with "sterling", again raising the point of marriage as a commercial, social transaction of status and wealth rather than of love, and accusing her of selling herself cheaply. She should "tender herself more dearly" – give herself with more care, and take care of herself. He finally uses the word to suggest she'll turn him into a fool, but also reminds of the phrase "tender-witted", meaning foolish or naïve.

CLOSE ANALYSIS

Polonius to Ophelia:
Ay, springes to catch woodcocks. I do know,
When the blood burns, how prodigal the soul
Lends the tongue vows: these blazes, daughter,
Giving more light than heat, extinct in both,
Even in their promise, as it is a-making,
You must not take for fire. From this time
Be somewhat scanter of your maiden presence;
Set your entreatments at a higher rate
Than a command to parley. For Lord Hamlet,
Believe so much in him, that he is young
And with a larger tether may he walk
Than may be given you: in few, Ophelia,
Do not believe his vows; for they are brokers,
Not of that dye which their investments show,
But mere implorators of unholy suits,
Breathing like sanctified and pious bawds,
The better to beguile. This is for all:
I would not, in plain terms, from this time forth,
Have you so slander any moment leisure,
As to give words or talk with the Lord Hamlet.
Look to't, I charge you: come your ways.

Ophelia: I shall obey, my lord.

There might be *some* sympathy in Polonius' acknowledgement that all young men "burn" when they are attracted to a woman, and will do anything to have her – but his daughter's wellbeing is most important. The metaphoric "giving more light than heat" symbolises the emptiness of Hamlet's words – the light is weak and will not warm her. The passion is a "blaze", burning hot and fast but very quickly burning itself out, not a "fire" which is more long-lasting (but still ultimately destructive).

The "tether" that restricts Hamlet is interesting in gender terms, an acknowledgement that he has more freedom than her – but he is still tethered. The blunt, almost brutal, "do not believe his vows" is an instruction that she must accept that despite any feelings he might profess he isn't free to marry her, as Laertes warned her as well, and that Hamlet is a typical youth – passionate when it suits but cold and will turn his back on her too.
Polonius accuses Hamlet of beguiling, lying – "like sanctified and pious bawds", the vulgar reference to prostitutes risking insulting Ophelia's honour.

He finally instructs her to stay away, and in a short, clipped tone she agrees with a formality of address – "my lord" – which makes us wonder if she is in agreement or simply doesn't know what else to say – he is her father after all.

ACT I SCENE 4

PLOT SUMMARY:

The scene moves to the platform at midnight where Hamlet is waiting for the ghost with Horatio and Marcellus. A noise within the castle disturbs them – Claudius celebrating his wedding. Hamlet's lengthy soliloquy about drunken customs is often cut from printed and performed editions – it's a digression into the national reputation of Denmark as badly behaved drunkards as a result of the king's excessive drinking. Perhaps this is a commentary on the role a monarch plays in a nation's reputation, as well as another way to negatively contrast Claudius with the previous King. The ghost appears – Hamlet questions whether it is from heaven or hell, but admits it looks like his father. Horatio begs him not to go, but of course he does. They decide to follow him, to keep him safe.

KEY THEMES:

Religion – is the ghost from heaven or hell? Hamlet questions it – but ultimately decides he doesn't need to know, just what it wants.

FORM, STRUCTURE AND LANGUAGE

"Angels and ministers of grace" speech includes imagery of religion, hell, death and heaven all intermingled.

The ghost– doesn't speak onstage in front of others; the staging of the ghost is tricky, especially in the Globe where the play's usually performed in daylight.

Hamlet's questioning to the ghost emphasises his desperation, his grief and loss over his father's death, and his desire to find something to justify his feelings.

KEY QUOTATIONS

Hamlet to the ghost: Bring with thee airs from heaven or blasts from hell,

Horatio:
What if it tempt you toward the flood, my lord,
Or to the dreadful summit of the cliff

...Which might deprive your sovereignty of reason
And draw you into madness? think of it:
The very place puts toys of desperation,
Without more motive, into every brain
That looks so many fathoms to the sea
And hears it roar beneath.

Foreshadowing the madness and destruction to come. Horatio seems to be the only one to see clearly the threat the ghost poses. He foretells Hamlet's madness, and the deaths at the end as they all are driving towards the cliff's edge. Olivier's 1948 version often uses the symbolic nature of Elsinore itself, high on a rocky cliff-side, to highlight the perilous nature of their actions.

Marcellus: Something is rotten in the state of Denmark.

But what exactly is it? A famous, incredibly versatile quote- is it Claudius, Gertrude, Hamlet, or the combination of them all together?

ACT 1 SCENE 5

PLOT SUMMARY:

The ghost and Hamlet are onstage alone. The ghost commands Hamlet to listen as he only has a short time before returning to Hell. The ghost tells Hamlet he was murdered by Claudius, his brother. He tells how Claudius found him sleeping, and poured a poison into his ear to kill him in the most painful way, which made his skin crust like leprosy. The ghost criticises Gertrude for adultery and incest, but tells Hamlet to leave *her* punishment to heaven and her own conscience, then he disappears.

In Hamlet's next soliloquy, he insists that he will remember his duty to his father and avenge his death, seeking justice for Claudius' actions. He vows to remember his father to the exclusion of all other responsibilities or thoughts.

Horatio and Marcellus catch up with him and persuade him to tell them what happened. Hamlet asks them to swear they will not reveal anything he tells them and the ghost, underneath the stage, three times adds his voice to his entreaty. They do swear, and he takes them offstage to tell them what he has heard.

KEY THEMES:

Religion: The ghost suggests he's from hell ("sulphurous and tormenting flames") because he died without confessing – an issue seen later when Hamlet refuses to kill Claudius for this reason.

Revenge: The ghost's command to Hamlet requires him to seek justice or vengeance – "howsoever thou pursuest this act," – but the difference between them is a source of debate for audiences: is Hamlet right to take the path that he does to serve justice, or is he seeking vengeance?

Father-son relationships: The ghost commands Hamlet as his father, and insists that he needs to remember him in an appropriate way. Contrast this with Claudius' suggestion that Hamlet's earlier grief is "unmanly", continuing too long and to intensely, and with the difficult authoritative relationship between Polonius and Laertes.

Appearance and reality as Hamlet realises the depths of Claudius' deception of them all.

FORM, STRUCTURE AND LANGUAGE

The ghost's first words to Hamlet are "mark me", highlighting the theme of filial (father-son) duty and responsibility as the ghost commands Hamlet, and continues through the scene to insist that he avenge the king's murder.

Sexual insults: The ghost adds to the accusations of Gertrude and Claudius' incest; the bed of Denmark is "a couch for lusty and damned incest", Gertrude is lowering herself to be with Claudius – "what a falling off was here!", lewd and "preying on garbage".

Staging: The Ghost speaks from beneath the stage "Swear!" – three times. This _could,_ if done badly be horribly funny rather than the slightly frightening and intimidating it seems more like it should be. In modern versions, it's often an eerie voice, manipulated and broadcast over the theatre sound system. But in The Globe, he is "beneath" – a specific stage direction. As there aren't many in Shakespeare, this one's worth remembering, as he's probably underneath the Globe's trapdoor and can be heard by the audience. (see Context, later, on original staging)

The end of the act: (see Form: Five act structure.) by this point, the initial set-up is complete – we're through the exposition, and just moving into rising action. We've met all the characters, the main conflict is established – Claudius has killed Hamlet's father and Hamlet must decide how to bring this to light and inflict punishment. Hamlet's final lines include another summative rhyming couplet – now that he knows everything is wrong, he needs to work out how he can solve the situation:

> The time is out of joint: O cursed spite,
> That ever I was born to set it right!

CONTEXT:

Religion – the ghost implies that he's coming from Hell, or Purgatory, because he wasn't able to confess before he died.

KEY QUOTATIONS

Ghost:
List, list, O, list!
If thou didst ever thy dear father love--
....Revenge his foul and most unnatural murder.

The ghost insists through the exclamation repetition and the emotive "foul and most unnatural" that it's Hamlet's duty to avenge him – along with a little bit of emotional blackmail suggesting if he doesn't avenge him, he never truly loved him.

Ghost
The serpent that did sting thy father's life
Now wears his crown.

Calling Claudius a "serpent" has connotations of evil, drawing on biblical imagery and the sibilant "sting" reinforces this. The final line is dramatic in its shortness.

Hamlet:
That one may smile, and smile, and be a villain;
At least I'm sure it may be so in Denmark:

The difference between appearance and reality is raised again – the play's theme of sight, and the unreliable nature of appearances is important in Claudius' deception of the court.

CLOSE ANALYSIS

Ghost
Ay, that incestuous, that adulterate beast,
With witchcraft of his wit, with traitorous gifts,--
O wicked wit and gifts, that have the power
So to seduce!--won to his shameful lust
The will of my most seeming-virtuous queen:
O Hamlet, what a falling-off was there!
From me, whose love was of that dignity
That it went hand in hand even with the vow
I made to her in marriage, and to decline
Upon a wretch whose natural gifts were poor
To those of mine!
But virtue, as it never will be moved,
Though lewdness court it in a shape of heaven,
So lust, though to a radiant angel link'd,
Will sate itself in a celestial bed,
And prey on garbage.

Thus was I, sleeping, by a brother's hand
Of life, of crown, of queen, at once dispatch'd:
Cut off even in the blossoms of my sin,
Unhousel'd, disappointed, unanel'd,
No reckoning made, but sent to my account
With all my imperfections on my head:
...

But, howsoever thou pursuest this act,
Taint not thy mind, nor let thy soul contrive
Against thy mother aught: leave her to heaven
And to those thorns that in her bosom lodge,
To prick and sting her.

Emotive insults of Claudius – "adulterate beast", "wicked" – show us his evil nature. Old Hamlet blames him for the 'seduction' of Gertrude, who is "seemingly virtuous" and appears to be absolved of the same responsibility. Certainly, the old King doesn't suggest that she has been previously adulterous or complicit in his murder.

The "falling off" implies she has fallen morally, as well as stooped to a lower level than she deserves. The old king venerates himself – he has "dignity" and genuinely loved her, but Claudius – his brother – is a "wretch", "poor" compared to him.

Gertrude is linked to celestial purity – the "celestial bed" and "radiant angel" – but even angels can fall to the depths.

The triadic "of life, of crown, of queen" *perhaps* suggests an order of importance – worth considering in a feminist interpretation to Gertrude's character. The king is "unhouse'd, disappointed, unanel'd" as he hasn't been able to confess and be absolved before he died, so he is condemned to Purgatory or even hell because of his mortal sins though the word "imperfections" downplays the severity of them.

Despite urging vengeance on Claudius, the king urges Hamlet not to "taint" his mind against his mother. The caesura emphasises the instruction "leave her to heaven" and her conscience to "prick and sting", the vicious verbs emphasising how she should feel. The old king seems to believe she is moral, but evidently Hamlet does not agree and condemns Gertrude's actions as the play continues.

ACT 2 SCENE I

PLOT SUMMARY:

In Polonius' house, where Polonius is instructing Reynaldo to keep watch over his son Laertes. It quickly becomes clear Polonius intends Reynaldo to spy on Laertes, to find out his behaviour and actions. He also tells Polonius to slander Laertes, telling his friends that he's heard rumours of debts, gambling, and so on, to see whether they defend him or agree. It's a risky suggestion – what if the rumours take hold? But Polonius insists this is the best way to discover people's true opinion of Laertes, to see whether they defend him or agree with stories of their own.

Reynaldo leaves and Ophelia comes in; she recounts an unseen-scene where Hamlet has aggressively addressed her, unkempt and wild-seeming, and has frightened her. Polonius interprets this as Hamlet being mad for Ophelia's love after she has – as commanded by him – refused to see Hamlet.

KEY THEMES:

Father/child relationships – Ophelia seeks Polonius' advice, and receives a different response this time. Polonius instructs his man to spy on Laertes – hardly the image of a loving, trusting father. It seems more likely that Polonius is concerned for family honour and reputation, and suspects that Laertes' behaviour away from home might cause rumour and scandal.

Love: Polonius believes Hamlet is 'mad with love' after being rejected by Ophelia.

FORM, STRUCTURE AND LANGUAGE

A new location – Polonius' house is one of the rare times we're outside "the castle" as a staging. Although in some cases it may be a suite of rooms within the castle, it seems it's actually separate as in Act 3 Hamlet commands the gates to be shut on Polonius when learning he's at home.

Polonius' forgetfulness – in speaking with Reynaldo, he forgets what he was about to say, implying that he is in fact an older courtier, and perhaps no longer functioning at his best, rather than a shrewd political advisor – which casts doubt on his other advice through the play.

An unseen scene: Ophelia recounts a scene to Polonius – by not permitting us to see it for ourselves, we have only Ophelia's description of it. She describes a mad Hamlet, unkempt, dishevelled, aggressive and very different to the despairing,

27

miserable Hamlet we have previously seen. However, we also know that he has conversed with his father's ghost and therefore the dramatic irony is that while Polonius thinks Hamlet is mad for love of Ophelia, we know that he is experiencing rage and guilt over his father's murder. It increases our sympathy for Ophelia, who is being manipulated by Polonius alternately to maintain the family honour or to help him into a further position of power, She's also previously appeared to be in love with Hamlet, yet has rejected him and must surely be upset about this encounter.

Secrets: Polonius says that to hide the difficulty Hamlet is experiencing would cause more grief than to discuss it. While this is to an extent self-serving – he's now in a position to see Hamlet as in love with his daughter and make their relationship closer, raising his family up – it also highlights the nature of secrecy in the play, which causes more problems than it can ever solve.

KEY QUOTATIONS

Ophelia:
He falls to such perusal of my face
As he would draw it. Long stay'd he so;
…He raised a sigh so piteous and profound
As it did seem to shatter all his bulk
The description of the impact of love is troubling; Hamlet is verging on mad. As an audience we know the depths of despair he's entered due to his father's ghost's revelations, but Ophelia has no such knowledge. The strong verb "shatter" against "all his bulk" emphasises how unhappy Hamlet is, and the depths of his melancholy.

Polonius:
Come, go with me: I will go seek the king.
This is the very ecstasy of love,
Whose violent property fordoes itself
And leads the will to desperate undertakings

Polonius is still commanding his daughter despite his apology for not believing Hamlet loved her – the declarative "come, go with me" gives her no further opportunity to explain what she believes Hamlet's feelings to be, or give her any say in what happens next. The juxtaposition of "ecstasy of love" and "violent" reminds us of both sides of love, and Polonius comments that it "leads the will to desperate undertakings" could be a tragic foreshadowing of Ophelia's death.

CLOSE ANALYSIS

Lord Polonius

That hath made him mad.
I am sorry that with better heed and judgment
I had not quoted him: I fear'd he did but trifle,
And meant to wreck thee; but, beshrew my jealousy!
By heaven, **it is as proper to our age**
To cast beyond ourselves in our opinions
As it is common for the younger sort
To lack discretion. Come, go we to the king:
This must be known; which, being kept close, might move
More grief to hide than hate to utter love

An unusually reflective comment from Polonius, who tends otherwise to see himself as wise and brook no discussion. He admits his fears that Hamlet would "trifle" with Ophelia and leave her not only broken hearted but ruined. His exclamative, "beshrew my jealousy!" suggests a wondering at himself, perhaps even anger – maybe that he has missed such an opportunity to get his daughter close to the heir to Denmark's throne.

His comment (in bold) implies a criticism of both old and young – the old think they know everything, and the young lack the restraint that comes with age.

His final two lines *could have* rhymed in Shakespeare's original pronunciation – the rhyming couplet this would form summarises his suggestion that to keep it secret would create more "grief" and trouble than if they discuss it openly. This could be taken as a critique of secrecy later in the play, especially as Polonius is often at the heart of some of the future secret meetings and plans that take place.

ACT 2 SCENE 2

PLOT SUMMARY:

Claudius and Gertrude welcome Rosencrantz and Guildenstern, who are Hamlet's friends – they have been invited partly to explain Hamlet's change in attitude. Gertrude adds her comment that Hamlet loves the two of them and they should help to find out what has altered him. They leave and Polonius enters – he tells Claudius he has discovered the cause of Hamlet's madness. Claudius must first see the ambassadors, so Polonius leaves. Claudius and Gertrude discuss Hamlet, Gertrude suggesting that Hamlet is upset by his father's death and their marriage, nothing more.

Polonius announces the ambassador Voltimand, who tells them that young Fortinbras of Norway had been raising an army against Denmark – but that when the old King of Norway heard, he was angry Fortinbras had acted without his agreement. The old king prevented Fortinbras carrying out his invasion, paid him an annual income and gave him permission to send his army against Poland instead – and has sent a letter asking permission for them to pass through Denmark on their way. Claudius agrees that this is good news, and he will reply later. The ambassadors leave.

Polonius tells them that he believes Hamlet is in love with Ophelia. They agree it is possible, and he tells them his plan. Hamlet's daily activities are well-known; Ophelia will come across him as it by accident, and Claudius and Polonius will be watching behind a curtain to see how he responds. They see him walking; Claudius and Gertrude leave, while Polonius addresses Hamlet.

Hamlet addresses him as a fishmonger, and their conversation is filled with statements that confuse Polonius. Is this evidence for Hamlet's madness, or that he is attempting to seem mad, so he can observe more closely? At the end of their conversation, Rosencrantz and Guildenstern arrive and greet Hamlet.

Their conversation with Hamlet is equally enigmatic. He tells them Denmark is a prison, and that they must be careful. He seems to know why they are there – his speech is again full of contradictions and plays on words that confuse and baffle them. He also says they were sent for, and must teach him why they are there.

They tell him there are some players/actors arrived to celebrate the king and queen's wedding, The players come across the three of them together, and Hamlet welcomes them. He seems to know them well, commenting that one

30

man is older and now growing a beard, and one lady is looking older. The main player recites a speech about the fall of Troy, impressing Hamlet, who instructs Polonius to see them to rooms in the castle. Hamlet agrees with the player that the company will perform The Murder of Gonzago the next night, with an additional speech that Hamlet will write to be inserted. He believes that this will make Claudius feel so guilty that he will give himself away, and Hamlet can have his revenge.

KEY THEMES:

Betrayal – Rosencrantz and Guildenstern lie to Hamlet from the beginning despite their apparent close friendship; they are summoned essentially to spy on him.

Madness: Hamlet's madness is discussed – and what it means to be mad. Polonius says "to define true madness, / What is't but to be nothing else but mad?" Hamlet admits to Rosencrantz and Guildenstern that he isn't mad, but in such mad language that they don't know whether to believe him, and Polonius is continually making reference to Hamlet being mad with love for Ophelia.

Love: Hamlet's letter to Ophelia is one of the most-used Shakespearean wedding quotes, for its romantic and heartfelt imagery.

Deception: Hamlet sets in motion the play-within-a-play which he hopes will provoke Claudius into revealing himself.

FORM, STRUCTURE AND LANGUAGE

Claudius' speech to Rosencrantz and Guildenstern – the royal inclusive pronoun "we" again used to signify Claudius' authority and control. His language is poetic and elevated as he suggests his concern for Hamlet's state of mind.

Commerce in Gertrude's welcome: She asks Rosencrantz and Guildenstern to "expend" their time "for the supply and profit of our hope", implying a commercial relationship between the two of them. She then promises "Your visitation shall receive such thanks / As fits a king's remembrance" – a fairly clear indication that they will be paid for their trouble.

Claudius and Gertrude's repetition: Claudius says "Thanks, Rosencrantz and gentle Guildenstern"; Gertrude follows with "Thanks, Guildenstern and gentle Rosencrantz". Is this a comic correction, implying that the two of them cannot be told apart? Or is it signifying that Claudius and Gertrude are in some respects as one, particularly in their outward, regal appearance.

31

Ophelia and celestial imagery: Hamlet's love letter uses imagery of the sun and stars to indicate the bright, joyful and permanent nature of his love, while Polonius admits he told Ophelia that Hamlet was "out of thy star", unable to marry her.

Polonius' asides show us what he is thinking but make mockery of him too because he seems to be missing the point of the conversation – he says he was nearly this mad for love, and that Hamlet is still concerned about Ophelia.

Hamlet's discussion with Polonius is spoken in prose rather than blank verse. Prose is often used for mundane subjects, or to signify that the character speaking is lower class – the gravediggers, for example – but here, Hamlet's prose indicates his madness, because he has not the wit or intellect to speak in blank verse. Yet again, is this deliberate on Hamlet's part to suggest that he is mad?

Sexual innuendo: Hamlet's conversation with Rosencrantz and Guildenstern is littered with sexual innuendo about fate's middle, waist, and private parts, with the ironic conclusion that fate is fickle.

Hamlet's intense questioning of Rosencrantz and Guildenstern again seems to suggest madness, because of its pace and speed, not allowing them to respond but seeming quite manic.

The ending: Hamlet's rhyming couplet: "the play 's the thing / Wherein I'll catch the conscience of the king." is another summation couplet; coming at the end of a soliloquy bemoaning Hamlet's lack of action. It launches the next act with a decisive movement, and a foreshadowing of what Hamlet hopes to achieve.

CONTEXT:

Travelling actors

KEY QUOTATIONS

Claudius:
What it should be,
More than his father's death, that thus hath put him
So much from the understanding of himself,
I cannot dream of:
Hamlet's state of mind is frequently discussed; here, madness is considered as being the lack of understanding of oneself, a disordered state compared to what he was before. Does Claudius pause after the caesura? He knows _a potential_

reason for Hamlet's change – is he suspicious or worried that Hamlet knows something?

Polonius

And I do think, or else this brain of mine
Hunts not the trail of policy so sure
As it hath used to do, that I have found
The very cause of Hamlet's lunacy.

Polonius alludes to his age here – the brain not "hunting" as well as it used to do (and of course, he is wrong, so the audience is aware he's not as reliable as he thinks himself). Through the blunt "lunacy" Polonius makes clear the subject of Hamlet's mental state has been the discussion of the court.

Gertrude:

I doubt it is no other but the main;
His father's death, and our o'erhasty marriage.

Here, Gertrude admits the quickness of their marriage – and that it has disturbed her son. That she uses "**o'er**" hasty perhaps suggests she regrets the speed of it, or at least the effect it has had on Hamlet.

Polonius:

What majesty should be, what duty is,
Why day is day, night night, and time is time,
Were nothing but to waste night, day and time.
Therefore, since **brevity is the soul of wit**,
And tediousness the limbs and outward flourishes,
I will be brief: your noble son is mad:
Mad call I it; for, to define true madness,
What is't but to be nothing else but mad?
But let that go.

The repetition of words here emphasises how full of nothing Polonius really is! He's saying it's no good making long speeches about what time, majesty, or madness is – and yet here he is doing almost exactly that. He does suggest that madness must be complete to be truly called such – "what is't but to be nothing else but mad?" The tangled confusion of this speech reflects Polonius' role as courtier; a gradually aging advisor who is often pompous, full of over-blown advice that he gives because he sees himself as wise.

'To the celestial and my soul's idol, the most
beautified Ophelia,'...
'Doubt thou the stars are fire;

Doubt that the sun doth move;
Doubt truth to be a liar;
But never doubt I love.

A letter from Hamlet – the hyperbolic, romanticised language heightens the emotion between the two of them. The repetition of "doubt," with its triadic structure followed by its opposite, is a romantic declaration of love. His use of the universal stars and sun also protests the depth and eternal nature of his love. There is an undertone in "doubt truth to be a liar" – considering the subjective nature of truth – which gives this pause, but the romance of it is undeniable. His use of "thou" is intimate and personal, and the heartfelt simplicity of the last line is beautiful.

Polonius:
'Lord Hamlet is a prince, out of thy star;
This must not be'

Recounting what he told Ophelia, Polonius echoes Hamlet's own celestial imagery but this time using it as a reason for them to remain separate, the different orbits they must make as one a prince and one in a lower social status.

Polonius:
And he, repulsed--a short tale to make--
Fell into a sadness, then into a fast,
Thence to a watch, thence into a weakness,
Thence to a lightness, and, by this declension,
Into the madness wherein now he raves,

Polonius' anaphoric use of "thence" makes the change in Hamlet seem inevitable – Ophelia's rejection has led to his current state, without a doubt. Love, therefore, leads to madness, but is helped along by "weakness" and "lightness", with an echo of Claudius' earlier criticism that Hamlet is "unmanly" in his grief: here, Polonius suggests that to be so in love is also "weak".

Polonius:
Though this be madness, yet there is method
in 't.

A suspicion that Hamlet isn't truly mad – there is a semblance of it in him still – and the audience might see even more than Polonius does. The alliterative quality has made this a memorable phrase, about seeking logic in the illogical.

Hamlet:
Why, then, 'tis none to you; for there is nothing
either good or bad, but thinking makes it so: to me

it is a prison.

The description of Denmark as a prison highlights Hamlet's internal agonies. The comment about thought is important in the rest of the play – is Hamlet right to seek vengeance? Should he have had a different approach / thought? If the ghost is thought to be from Hell then should he listen? Everything is about response, and attitude.

Hamlet: He that plays the king shall be welcome

A play on words; "plays" doesn't just mean act, but also to cause trouble for or interfere with.

Hamlet: I am but mad north-north-west: when the wind is
southerly I know a hawk from a handsaw.

A confession to Rosencrantz and Guildenstern that he is not mad – although he speaks truth, he does so in a way calculated to make them disbelieve it with the virtual nonsense of "north-north-west", and the alliterative "hawk from a handsaw" with its two completely unrelated objects.

Hamlet: God's bodykins, man, much better: use every man
after his desert, and who should 'scape whipping?

When Polonius says he'll treat the players as they deserve, Hamlet tells him to treat them better – as he would want to be treated, instead, because all men deserve punishment.

CLOSE ANALYSIS

Hamlet:
O God, I could be bounded in a nut shell and count
myself a king of infinite space, were it not that I
have bad dreams.
Guildenstern
Which dreams indeed are ambition, for the very
substance of the ambitious is merely the shadow of a dream.
Hamlet
A dream itself is but a shadow.
Rosencrantz
Truly, and I hold ambition of so airy and light a
quality that it is but a shadow's shadow.
Hamlet
Then are our beggars bodies, and our monarchs and
outstretched heroes the beggars' shadows. Shall we
to the court? for, by my fay, I cannot reason.

The confusion of dreams, ambition and shadow here suggest the confusion over Hamlet's madness. Hamlet states that "nothing is good or bad but thinking makes it so", and that he can be even in a nutshell, the smallest space, and feel trapped, because it's the dreams in his mind that torment him.

This begins as a reassurance that bad dreams are nothing but shadows. In the back and forth of the conversation, shadows, ambitions and dreams are all explained as being versions of one another, inverted and reinvented.

Hamlet then takes the concept further – kings and beggars are but mere shadows of one another, versions of each other: implying that the difference between them is perception, nothing more.

Hamlet:
What a piece of work is a man! how noble in reason! how infinite in faculty! in form and moving how express and admirable! in action how like an angel! an apprehension how like a god! the beauty of the world! the paragon of animals! And yet, to me, what is this quintessence of dust? man delights not me: no, nor woman neither, though by your smiling you seem to say so.

Unusually, this is spoken in prose rather than blank verse – perhaps suggesting again Hamlet's madness, but this also marks the normality and everyman nature of Hamlet's speech. The exclamation show the intense misery and anguish of his diatribe. He seems to admire mankind genuinely, with the hyperbolic language likening men to angels. His intense intellect and philosophical understanding is evident here in his understanding of the impressive nature of mankind. The comparatives put mankind in parallel with god and angels.

Yet, ultimately, Hamlet cannot find anything in man other than "dust", which brings to mind "ashes to ashes, dust to dust", Despite all their ability to think and their intellect, perhaps it's all a front and they really are just animals underneath it all.

Hamlet – final speech Act 2

O, what a rogue and peasant slave am I!
Is it not monstrous that this player here,
But in a fiction, in a dream of passion,
Could force his soul so to his own conceit
That from her working all his visage wann'd,
Tears in his eyes, distraction in's aspect,
A broken voice, and his whole function suiting
With forms to his conceit? and all for nothing!
For Hecuba!

Likening himself to a "peasant slave", the lowest possible man, Hamlet insults his own emotional and intellectual capacity. He finds it "monstrous" that the player can demonstrate such emotion, such "passion" for something fictional/ The player can summon "tears in his eyes, distraction in's aspect, a broken voice", a listing of woe and misery, yet it's "all for nothing" – emphasised on the end of the line. It's for a fictional character, nothing to him and nobody to weep for – "Hecuba" on its own line highlighting the despair of Hamlet that the player can find passion and misery for her and he can't seem to act properly

What's Hecuba to him, or he to Hecuba,
That he should weep for her? What would he do,
Had he the motive and the cue for passion
That I have? He would drown the stage with tears
And cleave the general ear with horrid speech,
Make mad the guilty and appal the free,
Confound the ignorant, and amaze indeed
The very faculties of eyes and ears. Yet I,
A dull and muddy-mettled rascal, peak,
Like John-a-dreams, unpregnant of my cause,
And can say nothing; no, not for a king,
Upon whose property and most dear life
A damn'd defeat was made. Am I a coward?
Who calls me villain? breaks my pate across?
Plucks off my beard, and blows it in my face?
Tweaks me by the nose? gives me the lie i' the throat,
As deep as to the lungs? who does me this?

The rhetorical question ("What would he do…..") suggests Hamlet questioning himself and his lack of action, the "cue for passion" which should be driving him forward in vengeance. He imagines the player's actions in hyperbolic and dramatic metaphors – "drown the stage with tears" – and parallelisms suggesting the breadth of his action – "make mad the guilty and appal the free", calling on the sense of the "faculties of eyes and ears" so that everyone would experience the same grief and anguish

Yet Hamlet does nothing. He is "dull and muddy-mettled", "can say nothing". He regrets that it's his father who's losing out by his inaction – the king has lost his life and experienced a "damn'd defeat", the harsh alliteration spat out in Hamlet's anger. He questions himself intensely and repeatedly, wishing for someone to accuses him of being a coward, a villain, someone who would challenge him, who "gives me the lie" so that he can no longer hesitate

Ha!
'Swounds, I should take it: for it cannot be

But I am pigeon-liver'd and lack gall
To make oppression bitter, or ere this
I should have fatted all the region kites
With this slave's offal: bloody, bawdy villain!
Remorseless, treacherous, lecherous, kindless villain!
O, vengeance!
Why, what an ass am I! This is most brave,
That I, the son of a dear father murder'd,
Prompted to my revenge by heaven and hell,
Must, like a whore, unpack my heart with words,
And fall a-cursing, like a very drab,
A scullion!

His language here expresses hatred against himself; the "pigeon-liver'd" implies pathetic, weak and useless while he wishes the "region kites" had preyed on him – the "bloody bawdy villain" is himself, ripped to pieces but those looking down on him for his inaction. This descends into a list of critical, emotive adjectives describing himself: "Remorseless, treacherous, lecherous, kindless" Hamlet's self-hatred is at its peak here, because he has not acted to avenge his father but instead has been moping about the castle wondering what to do about it.

He is "prompted to my revenge by heaven and hell", no longer wondering if the ghost is one or the other, he has convinced himself it comes from god and the devil, to have no opposition. He compares himself to a "whore" or "drab" or "scullion" (kitchen maid)– as at the beginning with "peasant slave" likening himself to the cheapest, most useless people he can imagine

Fie upon't! foh! About, my brain! I have heard
That guilty creatures sitting at a play
Have by the very cunning of the scene
Been struck so to the soul that presently
They have proclaim'd their malefactions;
For murder, though it have no tongue, will speak
With most miraculous organ. I'll have these players
Play something like the murder of my father
Before mine uncle: I'll observe his looks;
I'll tent him to the quick: if he but blench,
I know my course. The spirit that I have seen
May be the devil: and the devil hath power
To assume a pleasing shape; yea, and perhaps
Out of my weakness and my melancholy,
As he is very potent with such spirits,
Abuses me to damn me: I'll have grounds

More relative than this: the play 's the thing
Wherein I'll catch the conscience of the king.

Exit

He's heard that guilty men watching a play which reflects their own sins have been prompted to confess – and hopes Claudius will do the same. Murder might have "no tongue" but it will make itself heard through the conscience instead.

He will watch Claudius, and see if he "but blench" and look pale, as though he seems guilty, and then Hamlet will know what to do. This plan isn't as active as might have been assumed from his anger above. He still seems to need some further proof, beyond the ghost, suggesting he's still retaining some logical reason. He wonders if the spirit of his father is the devil in "a pleasing shape" and has no wish to go to hell, hut will try to entrap Claudius to find out for sure.

The anger is almost dismissed as being demonic – from his "weakness and melancholy" (that idea of weakness and an inappropriate response arising again) the devil "abuses me to damn me", making him feel angry enough to prompt him into a murder that would damn him to hell. But he does decide that he does need proof: the final rhyming couplet again sends us into the next act with a forward motion, a decision and a foreshadowing of Claudius' future behaviour.

ACT 3 SCENE I

PLOT SUMMARY:

In the castle, Claudius, Gertrude, Polonius, Ophelia, Rosencrantz and Guildenstern gather to discuss Hamlet. They say he admits he's distracted but won't tell them why. Claudius says he's pleased to hear that Hamlet is looking forward to the players, and he will attend the performance. Gertrude wishes Ophelia all the best with Hamlet.
Polonius tells Ophelia it's ironic that sometimes beauty and devotion cover up evil – and Claudius says in an aside that he feels the truth of that himself. Polonius and Claudius hide themselves behind the curtain, while Ophelia is walking – waiting for Hamlet. When he appears, she gives him back "remembrances" (letter?) that he sent to her. He denies giving her them, and they descend into an argument. He denies ever loving her, and tells her to get to a nunnery. He angrily denounces her, and indeed all marriages – decreeing that one half of every married couple should die. When he storms off, Claudius and Polonius agree that he's not in love, but mad for some other reason.

Claudius decides to send him to England to get him out of the way as his madness threatens the country. Polonius agrees, but asks Claudius to wait until after the play and give Gertrude an opportunity to talk to him first – Polonius will spy on them to see what they talk of.

KEY THEMES:

Deception: Ophelia is lying to Hamlet, and directed by her father. Claudius comments that he feels the guilt of maintaining a façade against everyone. Polonius arranges spying first on Ophelia and Hamlet, and then on Hamlet and Gertrude.

Love: Hamlet denies ever loving Ophelia, but is it true? The way this is delivered can make all the difference. If he did love her, does he know he's being watched and feel betrayed? Does the audience blame him for Ophelia's swift decline?

FORM, STRUCTURE AND LANGUAGE

Claudius' aside – How smart a lash that speech doth give my conscience! When Polonius says devotion covers the devil's actions, Claudius seems to be feeling the truth of it – a moment of confession to the audience that implies he genuinely feels guilty over his actions.

Hamlet's accusations against women are vicious and violent, indicating his misogynistic attitude – or his rage at his mother spilling over into his relationship with Ophelia.

Rhyming couplet at the end: "It shall be so: / Madness in great ones must not unwatch'd go" – Claudius this time summarises the scene, often alone onstage to himself or the audience – as he's planning to send Hamlet away, claiming to protect the nation but the dramatic irony is that the audience know he is protecting himself.

CONTEXT:

Role of women – The treatment of Ophelia by Hamlet

KEY QUOTATIONS

Claudius on Hamlet: With turbulent and dangerous lunacy?

Gertrude on Hamlet: Nor do we find him forward to be sounded, / But, with a crafty madness, keeps aloof,

Gertrude to Ophelia:

And for your part, Ophelia, I do wish
That your good beauties be the happy cause
Of Hamlet's wildness: so shall I hope your virtues
Will bring him to his wonted way again

The reference to beauty and virtue shows what is prized in relationships and marriage, and the age-old "fairy-tale' that a woman can 'tame' a man gone bad. It's one of the few times Ophelia is addressed by someone else; often the political discussions are continued over her head, almost, and it's only here that Gertrude speaks to her, as a woman speaking to her future daughter in law.

Polonius to Ophelia:

that with devotion's visage
And pious action we do sugar o'er
The devil himself.

The conflict of devotion/pious and the devil here imply the conflict that Claudius is experiencing (as he himself notes in an aside). To "sugar o'er", to cover up something sinful in something sweet, is a common theme of the play – the "serpent" hiding, for example, until the moment it strikes. It's also a disturbing comment on how easy it is to "smile and smile and play the villain" and nobody will be any the wiser.

Hamlet: I did love you once.

The simplicity of this statement lends it its beauty, and the way this is played can dramatically alter our impression of Hamlet – is he shouting, angry at her deception, or heartbroken, touching her for the last time? She's already rejected him but does he really know why? There are so many missing scenes in *Hamlet*, that we can only speculate – and show it through the actions of the actor playing him.

Hamlet: I have heard of your paintings too, well enough; God
has given you one face, and you make yourselves
another: you jig, you amble, and you lisp, and
nick-name God's creatures, and make your wantonness
your ignorance.

Hamlet describes women as practicing constant deception, painting their faces to hide what is underneath. The list of verbs (jig, amble, lisp) making women seem weak, childish and simpering, but actually, Hamlet argues, these attitudes are a deliberate façade designed to entrap men. Hamlet seems torn; he doesn't believe women are honest anymore, and can only see them as hiding something. The reference to "wantonness" again reveals his obsession with sexual misdeeds of Gertrude, and linking Ophelia to the same behaviour he suspects of his mother.

Ophelia on Hamlet's madness: Like sweet bells jangled, out of tune and harsh;

ACT 3 SCENE 2

PLOT SUMMARY:

Hamlet meets with the actors, and instructs the First Player how to deliver the speech that Hamlet has writing for him. The court, including Horatio, arrive to watch the performance. Hamlet and Claudius exchange words which leave Claudius baffled. Hamlet also sexually insults Ophelia with his innuendo.

The players come onstage and perform, silently, their drama – the murder of King Hamlet. They present Gertrude/Queen as a loving wife, who is reluctant to marry afterwards, but does eventually concede. Throughout the play, Hamlet speaks to Gertrude and Claudius to see how they are reacting to the play in front of them. When it gets to the moment poison is poured in the King's ear, Gertrude asks Claudius what is wrong – he calls for light, and everyone except Hamlet and Horatio exit. Hamlet takes the king's exit and disturbance as proof of his guilt.

Rosencrantz and Guildenstern return, and ask Hamlet to go speak with his mother in her chamber. Polonius comes on and reiterates the summons; Hamlet is left alone onstage. He speaks a soliloquy – he will be "cruel but not unnatural", and in speaking with his mother will be cold and heartless, but will not injure her.

KEY THEMES:

Acting and deception – the player is told how to deliver an effective, dramatic speech – how to pretend well.

Appearance and reality – the players perform the act of the murder we did not see at the beginning of the play.

Revenge – Hamlet uses the play as a means to make Claudius confess

FORM, STRUCTURE AND LANGUAGE

Prose – Hamlet speaks to the players in prose, as they are lower status characters than he is, and so he communicates with them using their style.

Play within a play – the framed play portrays the murder of King Hamlet.

CONTEXT:

Stagecraft – the comments Hamlet makes on how to deliver the speech have a comic irony onstage, as he describes the way a bad actor can ruin a good speech,

KEY QUOTATIONS

Claudius: I have nothing with this answer, Hamlet; these words are not mine.
Hamlet: No, nor mine now.
Here, Claudius is bewildered – and dismissive – of Hamlet's apparent lack of sense (referring to being a chameleon and eating the air) – but immediately Hamlet makes a play on words which belies his madness and reveals that he is still very much in control – the words indeed are not his for they have been given to the player to speak.

Hamlet: Why, look you now, how unworthy a thing you make of me! You would play upon me; you would seem to know my stops; you would pluck out the heart of my mystery; you would sound me from my lowest note to the top of my compass: and there is much music, excellent voice, in this little organ; yet cannot you make it speak. 'Sblood, do you think I am easier to be played on than a pipe? Call me what instrument you will, though you can fret me, yet you cannot play upon me.
The language of musical instruments is perhaps odd here; the "stops", "pluck out the heart", "sound me" and so on makes Hamlet seem something that is played – manipulated, toyed with, and used. Yet while an instrument would usually give pleasure to the player, Hamlet argues that he is impossible to play fully and will not be cooperative; they may "fret" and worry, use and manipulate him, but they will never completely succeed in "playing" him.

CLOSE ANALYSIS

Hamlet: Lady, shall I lie in your lap? _Lying down at OPHELIA's feet_ **Ophelia:** No, my lord. **Hamlet:** I mean, my head upon your lap? **Ophelia:** Ay, my lord. **Hamlet:** Do you think I meant country matters? **Ophelia:** I think nothing, my lord.	This speech is full of sexual innuendo – "country matters" is slang for sex, and lying in her lap is a fairly direct reference Ophelia appears shocked from her exclamation – is her "I think nothing" a way to stop him speaking of this, to hide her embarrassment, or is there any

Hamlet: That's a fair thought to lie between maids' legs. **Ophelia:** What is, my lord? **Hamlet:** Nothing. **Ophelia:** You are merry, my lord. **Hamlet:** Who, I? **Ophelia:** Ay, my lord. **Hamlet:** O God, your only jig-maker. What should a man do but be merry? for, look you, how cheerfully my mother looks, and my father died within these two hours. **Ophelia:** Nay, 'tis twice two months, my lord. **Hamlet:** So long? Nay then, let the devil wear black, for I'll have a suit of sables. O heavens! die two months ago, and not forgotten yet? Then there's hope a great man's memory may outlive his life half a year: but, by'r lady, he must build churches, then; or else shall he suffer not thinking on, with the hobby-horse, whose epitaph is 'For, O, for, O, the hobby-horse is forgot.' …. **Ophelia:** You are keen, my lord, you are keen. **Hamlet:** It would cost you a groaning to take off my edge.	possibility she might be flirting? The "you are merry" comment could be either a repressive put-down, or a warm encouragement. Hamlet dismisses of women – Gertrude is happy despite her recent widowing (although Ophelia seems to think four months is adequate?) There's also a jibe back to the mourning clothes of Act 1, when Hamlet says "the devil wear black", and he'll wear a slightly lighter colour of sable (light brown). Hamlet comments that a man should build a church to maintain his memory, for he can't trust a woman to do it. The final comment here is Hamlet again with a sexual innuendo that Ophelia will be able to "take off my edge" with a "groaning" – quite explicit, really!

ACT 3 SCENE 3

PLOT SUMMARY:

Claudius tells Rosencrantz and Guildenstern that they must take Hamlet to England. Polonius returns, and tells Claudius that he will hide behind the arras/curtain while Gertrude and Hamlet speak, and then will report back to Claudius. When alone, Claudius begins to soliloquise, exploring the fact that he knows he should feel guilty – but how can he, when he still enjoys the "spoils" of his crime? He appears to be confused, maybe even anguished, by his inability to pray for forgiveness for something he continues to benefit from. While he's there, Hamlet comes in unseen – and starts as if to kill Claudius, but hesitates. If he kills him now, he may go to heaven. Instead, Hamlet decides to wait until a moment he can be certain that Claudius will go to hell.

KEY THEMES:

Secrecy and deception – Polonius' plan to hide himself in Gertrude's chamber emphasises his political role at court. Claudius has set in motion the plot to kill Hamlet.

FORM, STRUCTURE AND LANGUAGE

Claudius' soliloquy – the king speaks in blank verse as he attempts to pray and unburden his soul in the scene, which is usually played in a chapel because of the prayer-like nature of the speech.

Staging: Directors need to make Hamlet's entrance – and Claudius not noticing – seem natural. Many modern film directors give Hamlet his soliloquy as a voiceover instead (the David Tennant version, for example), while other onstage versions might have Hamlet further away and rely on the audience suspending disbelief.

CONTEXT:

Religion: the fact that Claudius is attempting, at least, to pray is indication of the level of general faith in the time – yet he admits that he can't. Hamlet's pause is also religiously-inspired: his logic is that he believes Claudius to be praying, and therefore in a state of grace – to kill him now would send him to heaven, something denied his own father. Instead, true vengeance demands that he waits until Claudius; soul is blackened, and therefore he will be sent to hell instead.

KEY QUOTATIONS

Claudius: I like him not, nor stands it safe with us
To let his madness range.
Is this an excuse to get rid of Hamlet and protect himself, or does Claudius have at least some genuine regard for the wellbeing of Denmark? Which threat is he trying to remove here?

Rosencrantz: The cease of majesty
Dies not alone; but, like a gulf, doth draw
What's near it with it
To Claudius, this seems sympathetic – the role of a king is important: he guides

the kingdom's fortune and, where he goes, so goes the kingdom – even according to his mood. Perhaps Shakespeare is making a broader comment about political leadership too, and the responsibility that leaders have in making good decisions for those who go along with them.

Hamlet:
am I then revenged,
To take him in the purging of his soul,
When he is fit and season'd for his passage?
....
Then trip him, that his heels may kick at heaven,
And that his soul may be as damn'd and black
As hell, whereto it goes.

Hamlet's ironically unaware that Claudius is far from grace – his inability to pray means he can't be forgiven for his crime, so had Hamlet acted now then he would have gone to hell. The "purging of his soul" hasn't happened, and Claudius is spiritually trapped in a state of despair. The imagery of Claudius diving into hell, heels "kicking" at heaven. "Damned and black" indicates the depths of Hamlet's desire for revenge – he not only wants to murder Claudius but to murder him in such a way that his eternal soul will also suffer. Ironically, this would condemn Hamlet to a similar fate as only God is permitted to exact this kind of justice.

CLOSE ANALYSIS

This scene forms the highpoint of tension in the play as Claudius' guilt is exposed, and Hamlet fails to take his revenge. Claudius admits to murder here, confirming what the audience has previously heard from the ghost.

Claudius' soliloquy:

O, my offence is rank it smells to heaven;
It hath the primal eldest curse upon't,
A brother's murder. Pray can I not,
Though inclination be as sharp as will:
My stronger guilt defeats my strong intent;
And, like a man to double business bound,
I stand in pause where I shall first begin,
And both neglect. What if this cursed hand
Were thicker than itself with brother's blood,
Is there not rain enough in the sweet heavens
To wash it white as snow? Whereto serves mercy

Claudius is aware of his offence – "it smells to heaven" and he's reminded of Cain, the biblical son of Adam who killed his brother Abel, committing mankind's first murder. He "stands in pause" because he's in the chapel yet unable to pray properly – he doesn't seem to *really* feel the guilt he knows that he should. The reference to the "cursed hand" covered in blood that can't be washed clean is an image reused elsewhere in Shakespeare's career, in Lady Macbeth's speech. The rain "white as snow", the colour of innocence and symbolic of a baptism, isn't enough to remove his sin from his soul.

But to confront the visage of offence?
And what's in prayer but this two-fold force,
To be forestalled ere we come to fall,
Or pardon'd being down? Then I'll look up;
My fault is past. But, O, what form of prayer
Can serve my turn? 'Forgive me my foul murder'?
That cannot be; since I am still possess'd
Of those effects for which I did the murder,
My crown, mine own ambition and my queen.
May one be pardon'd and retain the offence?
In the corrupted currents of this world
Offence's gilded hand may shove by justice,
And oft 'tis seen the wicked prize itself
Buys out the law: but 'tis not so above;
There is no shuffling, there the action lies
In his true nature; and we ourselves compell'd,

Claudius' rhetorical questions suggest he's struggling somewhat with the idea, but is it his conscience or his lack of it? He says he's still "possessed" of what he won from the murder: "my crown, mine own ambition and my queen". The triad puts the crown and country first and Gertrude last, but the repetition of my/mine suggests he's not about to give these up any time soon.

Even to the teeth and forehead of our faults,
To give in evidence. What then? what rests?
Try what repentance can: what can it not?
Yet what can it when one can not repent?
O wretched state! O bosom black as death!
O limed soul, that, struggling to be free,
Art more engaged! Help, angels! Make assay!
Bow, stubborn knees; and, heart with strings of steel,
Be soft as sinews of the newborn babe!
All may be well.

Retires and kneels

He knows that in heaven "above" there will be another type of reckoning, a different justice he can't escape – "there the action lies in his true nature" – and he will have to face his consequences sometime.

Yet, the further questions and exclamations show that he can't feel the guilt and conscience that he should. He calls himself "wretched", "black", and bemoans his "limed soul", rotting and trapped in his mortal sin, then calls out the angels for guidance.

He kneels, to attempt to pray, and Hamlet enters unseen. Hamlet's soliloquy (edited out in the section below) is often in modern film adaptations performed as a voiceover, to explain the fact that Claudius doesn't hear him. In a theatre, we have to suspend disbelief.

Enter HAMLET

[Hamlet's interjected soliloquy[

[Rising] My words fly up, my thoughts remain below:
Words without thoughts never to heaven go.

The final rhyming couplet of the scene has the parallelism of the two lines connecting heaven and hell. Claudius; thoughts "remain below" – is this on earth or in hell? The separation of "words" and "thoughts" also shows that he can't genuinely mean a confession; he can say the words but he can't ever truly ask for forgiveness – this irony is compounded by the fact that Hamlet's just decided not to kill him because he thinks Claudius has confessed and, forgiven, would go to heaven not hell.

ACT 3 SCENE 4

PLOT SUMMARY:

In Gertrude's "closet" (her rooms in the castle), Polonius instructs her in the plan. She agrees, and Polonius hides behind the arras, likely a large tapestry on the wall. Hamlet immediately is confrontational with Gertrude, twisting her words and accusing her of incest and betraying his father. With his anger, she's afraid he means to murder her, and shouts for help. Polonius shouts from behind the arras and Hamlet stabs him. Gertrude is distraught, calling it a bloody deed – he replies as bloody as to kill a king and marry his brother which shocks her – perhaps confirming she had no idea about the murder?

Hamlet starts to verbally abuse his mother, excoriating her for having married so hastily and being sexually voracious. She tries to defend herself and remind him that, as his mother, she deserves his respect. Even when she tries to say she realises how sinful she is, he continues to attack her. Then, the ghost enters – but only Hamlet can see him. The ghost instructs him to speak more kindly to Gertrude, not castigate her, reminding Hamlet that his purpose was to have revenge on Claudius, not on Gertrude. Hamlet's speaking to the ghost, however, and trying to point him out to his mother, convinces Gertrude that he is mad indeed. Even when he says he sees King Hamlet, she tells him it's the product of grief and madness, not reality.

Hamlet tells Gertrude to no longer sleep with Claudius, and become more virtuous. He says he regrets killing Polonius, but heaven must have willed his death. Hamlet also says that he is commanded to go to England – but he knows that Rosencrantz and Guildenstern are not to be trusted. He says farewell and leaves, dragging out Polonius' body.

KEY THEMES:

Sexuality and role of women – Hamlet's reaction to Gertrude continues to be more and more extreme. He castigates her for having a sexual appetite 'at her age' and accuses her of simply being voracious, rather than having any thought that she loves Claudius.

FORM, STRUCTURE AND LANGUAGE

Hamlet's verbal attack on Gertrude – littered with rhetorical questions and fragmented utterances indicating his anger at Gertrude, and he doesn't let her speak until he seems exhausted by his rage.

The ghost's interruption abruptly changes the scene: is Hamlet frightened here, defiant, or ashamed that he hasn't yet done as his father asked?

CONTEXT:

Expectations of women, especially widows and older women

KEY QUOTATIONS

Queen Gertrude: Hamlet, thou hast thy father much offended.
Hamlet: Mother, you have my father much offended.
Queen Gertrude: Come, come, you answer with an idle tongue.

Hamlet: Go, go, you question with a wicked tongue.

Hamlet's play on words, twisting his mother's comments, indicate his sanity rather than his madness – he is still intelligent enough to manipulate his language in this way, maintaining such an opaque distance between the two of them that she can't but become frustrated with him.

Hamlet: A bloody deed! almost as bad, good mother,
As kill a king, and marry with his brother.

Rhyming draws attention to the accusation, the blunt nature of "kill a king" is also important as here Hamlet isn't hedging his words or hiding under manipulative language. This is his moment of accusation, and Gertrude responds with simple confusion.

Hamlet: Such an act
That blurs the grace and blush of modesty,
Calls virtue hypocrite, takes off the rose

Hamlet's misogyny coming through again? Or is this very specifically aimed at his mother alone? The reference to the "rose" is a perversion of the clichéd symbol of romance, as the rose is removed and replaced with a stain instead. The contradictory "virtue hypocrite" suggests how closely the two may be, and how easy it becomes to go from one to the other.

Hamlet: Could you on this fair mountain leave to feed,
And batten on this moor?

Comparing the king – the fair mountain, with connotations of regality and natural majestic beauty – with the "moor" Claudius, harsh, scrubby, unforgiving and often considered to be plain, inhospitable to the creatures living on it. Like the earlier "Hyperion to a satyr" comment, Hamlet venerates his father and criticises his uncle – and therefore criticising his mother's choice to go from one to the other.

Hamlet: You cannot call it love; for at your age
The hey-day in the blood is tame

Another bitter accusation to Gertrude, this time that she is too old to have a sexual appetite, and should have remained unmarried which would have been more decorous. He flatly refuses to believe Gertrude in love and the audience is left in a quandary: she never *says* that they are, but Hamlet never gives her an opportunity to defend herself.

Gertrude: [inside my soul] there I see such black and grained spots
As will not leave their tinct

Although Gertrude seems to be admitting the sin in the "black" spots which are "grained" and therefore permanent, is she perhaps trying to calm Hamlet by agreeing with him? Very much this depends on the director's interpretation, and whether they want Gertrude to be sympathetic, and how aggressive Hamlet is. There's also an interesting parallel with Claudius' prayer scene when he says that his "cursed hand" is so covered in blood there is "not rain enough…to wash it white", maintaining the same engrained, bloodied and sinful appearance as Gertrude imagines her soul to be.

Hamlet: to live
In the rank sweat of an enseamed bed,
Stew'd in corruption
The disturbing, physically disgusting nature of this description attacks Gertrude's sexuality. With its fetid, unsavoury description, Hamlet makes Claudius and Gertrude's relationship seem tawdry and dirty.

The ghost: this visitation
Is but to whet thy almost blunted purpose
The ghost arrives to put Hamlet back on track as he's at risk of becoming distracted by Gertrude, particularly having just decided not to kill Claudius. The "whet" suggests to sharpen and bring to a point, as a whetstone does a sword.

Hamlet: My pulse, as yours, doth temperately keep time,
And makes as healthful music: it is not madness
Hamlet protests to his mother that he's not mad. Interestingly he refers to their "temperate" natures, a description at odds with the lascivious lustful attitudes he's accusing her of having. Here, madness is purely physical and can be proven through the health of the body.

Gertrude: O Hamlet, thou hast cleft my heart in twain.
A distraught exclamation from Gertrude, devastated by his accusation – which she does seem to believe almost immediately (she doesn't question him on any details, but accepts what he is saying). Is she "cleft" in "twain" because of Claudius' deception? Or does she in fact believe Hamlet mad and is trying to assuage his anger?

Hamlet: my two schoolfellows,
Whom I will trust as I will adders fang'd,
The deception of Rosencrantz and Guildenstern hasn't gone unnoticed by Hamlet, but he's curious enough to let the voyage to England play out to see what will happen. The reference to snakes – "adders" – is symbolic of evil.

ACT 4 SCENE 1

PLOT SUMMARY:

Claudius and Gertrude are alone together. She tells him that she fears Hamlet is "mad as the sea and wind" and that he has killed Polonius. Claudius says that it would have been him, if he had been there (why does he think Hamlet wants him dead?) and uses this to suggest to Gertrude that Hamlet must be sent away. He claims he would have done it sooner except for the love he has for Hamlet. Gertrude tells Claudius that Hamlet has taken the body away and weeps in regret. Claudius sends Rosencrantz and Guildenstern to find Hamlet, and Polonius' body, and bring them to the chapel.

KEY THEMES:

Deception – Gertrude lies to Claudius about Hamlet's weeping for Polonius – is she protecting her son because she believes he's right about Claudius being a murderer? Or simply because he's her son?

Madness – Gertrude blames Hamlet's madness for Polonius' death.

FORM, STRUCTURE AND LANGUAGE

Ending with a rhyming couple – the final lines from Claudius leave a lasting impression of doom, and from this point on the action moves swiftly towards the resolution of the play.

KEY QUOTATIONS

Claudius:
It will be laid to us, whose providence
Should have kept short, restrain'd and out of haunt,
This mad young man: but so much was our love,
We would not understand what was most fit;
But, like the owner of a foul disease,
To keep it from divulging, let it feed
Even on the pith of Life.

The imagery of a disease, allowed to flourish and spread, is an interesting one to use in the context of madness; Elizabethans weren't always sure whether it was a mental or physical illness. He refers to Hamlet as being 'owned', acknowledging his own responsibility (to some extent) in Hamlet's change and, alone with Gertrude, seems to be pitying of Hamlet. It's up to an audience (and a director) to determine how much they think Claudius is genuine at any point; does he feel sympathy for Hamlet and think his madness genuine, or does he see Hamlet as a more knowing and deliberate threat to him?

Gertrude: he weeps for what is done
Gertrude protects Hamlet. There's been no evidence of his being upset or angry over Polonius' death, and so telling Claudius this makes it seem as though he is either regretful or mad indeed.

Claudius: Come, Gertrude, we'll call up our wisest friends;
And let them know, both what we mean to do,
And what's untimely done. O, come away!
My soul is full of discord and dismay.
The harsh consonants of "discord and dismay" set the tone for what is to come, foreshadowing the darkness that's settling over Denmark. Polonius' death, like the old Hamlet's, is "untimely done". The exclamation perhaps could be interpreted to suggest that Gertrude is reluctant to follow – if she believes Hamlet completely, that would make sense as she would be tentative and nervous around Claudius now.

ACT 4 SCENE 2

PLOT SUMMARY:

Rosencrantz and Guildenstern find Hamlet, who evades their questioning and speaks riddles to persuade them further of his madness. He tells them to bring him to Claudius.

ACT 4 SCENE 3

PLOT SUMMARY:

Claudius knows he must remove Hamlet, but will struggle because Hamlet is still so popular. Rosencrantz nd Guildenstern bring him back to face Claudius. Hamlet antagonises Claudius, telling him that a beggar and a king are the same (see Close Analysis), but eventually says that Polonius' body is in the lobby. Claudius sends servants to fetch the body to the chapel.

Claudius tells Hamlet that he will be sent to England. Hamlet agrees, and in a final jab calls Claudius "mother" – arguing that because they are married and now 'one flesh', they are interchangeable.

When Hamlet has gone, Rosencrantz and Guildenstern follow after. Claudius, in a soliloquy spoken 'to England', says that he is sending Hamlet with letters that ask England to kill Hamlet on his behalf.

KEY THEMES:

Deception – Claudius claims to be sending Hamlet to England to protect him from punishment. He then secretly sends letters asking the English authorities to kill Hamlet.

FORM, STRUCTURE AND LANGUAGE

Claudius' soliloquy– reveals the true intent behind sending Hamlet to England so the audience is waiting (dramatic irony) for Hamlet to discover the deception.

KEY QUOTATIONS

Claudius about Hamlet:
He's loved of the distracted multitude,
Who like not in their judgment, but their eyes....
This sudden sending him away must seem
Deliberate pause: diseases desperate grown
By desperate appliance are relieved,
Or not at all.
Again Claudius uses the language of disease to express his feelings about Hamlet's dangerous attitudes and the way that it can spread. He sees himself as more logical and rational than the people who like with "their eyes", and perhaps it's this superiority that has led Claudius to the murder of his brother too. The sending away must be "deliberate pause" with the caesura after the phrase, while Claudius comes to the conclusion that Hamlet must be removed by "desperate appliance" – any means necessary.

CLOSE ANALYSIS

Hamlet:
Not where he eats, but where he is eaten: a certain convocation of politic worms are e'en at him. Your worm is your only emperor for diet: we fat all creatures else to fat us, and we fat ourselves for maggots: your fat king and your lean beggar is but variable service, two dishes, but to one table: that's the end.

> A man may fish with the worm that hath eat of a
> king, and cat of the fish that hath fed of that worm.

> Nothing but to show you how a king may go a
> progress through the guts of a beggar

Hamlet's musing on the equality of man – after death, all are equal. "We fat ourselves…maggots" implies that no matter what, we're all part of the circle of life, and all return to the ground once we are dead – until we feed the soil, the vegetables and grass, and then animals and others. Thus, it doesn't matter, this internal games of politics that Denmark is playing, because we are all, in the end, equal. It's interesting Hamlet doesn't relate this to religion, but instead seems rather tired of the whole thing, and doubtful of its point.

Claudius:
> Since yet thy cicatrice looks raw and red
> After the Danish sword, and thy free awe
> Pays homage to us--thou mayst not coldly set
> Our sovereign process; which imports at full,
> By letters congruing to that effect,
> The present death of Hamlet. Do it, England;
> For like the hectic in my blood he rages,
> And thou must cure me: till I know 'tis done,
> Howe'er my haps, my joys were ne'er begun.

The "cicatrice" or scar is raw – Claudius is alluding to a wound inflicted by Denmark on England in a recent battle. In his letter to England, arranging Hamlet's death, he both threatens and pleads with them. He argues that they should "pay homage", and remember the hurt Denmark is capable of doing. He also refers again to Hamlet as being a disease or plague ("in my blood he rages") and that he needs curing; elsewhere the madness is threatening to overwhelm the whole of Denmark. Claudius again positions himself as being Denmark itself.

ACT 4 SCENE 4

PLOT SUMMARY:

Prince Fortinbras returns to the plot. The Captain of his army meets Hamlet, and tells him (and reminds the audience!) what Fortinbras is doing in Denmark. The Captain says they're going for nothing more than honour – which pricks

Hamlet's conscience further and, in another soliloquy, Hamlet says that this is the final straw: he really must act now, or he is worth nothing.

KEY THEMES:

Honour and duty – the army Hamlet meets is led by Fortinbras, heading to invade Poland simply for Norway's honour. While a modern audience might find the idea of war for honour an unpalatable one, the idea is enough to make Hamlet reconsider his _own_ definition of honour and how he is failing to live up to his father's final request of him.

FORM, STRUCTURE AND LANGUAGE

Return of Fortinbras – for most of the play, Fortinbras is a shadowy off-stage rumour. Now he appears, with an army at his back. He's been talked about earlier (last in Act 2 scene 2) as being equal to Hamlet, but wanting to lead an army for honour and the good of Norway. He's on his way to conquer Poland, and passing through Denmark to get there.

KEY QUOTATIONS

Captain: We go to gain a little patch of ground
That hath in it no profit but the name
There's nothing in Poland except "the name" they will gain for themselves, the honour and fame of being the ones to defeat it.

CLOSE ANALYSIS

Hamlet:

How all occasions do inform against me,
And spur my dull revenge! What is a man,
If his chief good and market of his time
Be but to sleep and feed? a beast, no more.
Sure, he that made us with such large discourse,
Looking before and after, gave us not
That capability and god-like reason
To fust in us unused. Now, whether it be
Bestial oblivion, or some craven scruple
Of thinking too precisely on the event,
A thought which, quarter'd, hath but one part wisdom
And ever three parts coward, I do not know

Why yet I live to say 'This thing's to do;'
Sith I have cause and will and strength and means
To do't. Examples gross as earth exhort me:
Witness this army of such mass and charge
Led by a delicate and tender prince,
Whose spirit with divine ambition puff'd
Makes mouths at the invisible event,
Exposing what is mortal and unsure
To all that fortune, death and danger dare,
Even for an egg-shell. Rightly to be great
Is not to stir without great argument,
But greatly to find quarrel in a straw
When honour's at the stake. How stand I then,
That have a father kill'd, a mother stain'd,
Excitements of my reason and my blood,
And let all sleep? while, to my shame, I see
The imminent death of twenty thousand men,
That, for a fantasy and trick of fame,
Go to their graves like beds, fight for a plot
Whereon the numbers cannot try the cause,
Which is not tomb enough and continent
To hide the slain? O, from this time forth,
My thoughts be bloody, or be nothing worth!

Having just spoken to the captain, who informs him that Fortinbras is about to invade Poland for nothing more than the honour of conquest, Hamlet is struck with shame and guilt at his own lack of honourable action. His rhetorical "what is man?" encompasses the idea that man but do *something* to be more than a beast. Men have "god-like reason", using his imagination and thought is essential to ensure that he is more than a mere animal – perhaps ironic as the action he wishes to take is arguably simple violence against another, not thought-provoked at all. His *lack* of action is "bestial oblivion or some craven scruple", implying that to scruple, or hesitate with thought is cowardly, and not worthy of a prince.

He calls himself coward once more, with the phrase "cause and will and strength and means" an overwhelming list which loads upon him the reasons why he should commit murder in his father's name. Fortinbras is described as "delicate and tender" but with "divine ambition", an honourable and respectable example.

The soliloquy moves onto talk of "greatness" and how he becomes great, rather than either a mere animal or (worse?) a coward. He argues greatness is not killing for the sake of it – perhaps like Fortinbras? – but Hamlet has plenty of genuine reasons for a grievance. "a father killed, a mother stain'd", with again the reference to Gertrude as being a major motivating factor in his desire for revenge. The argument that he "lets all sleep" brings to mind the "to be or not to be" soliloquy when he says, "to sleep, perchance to dream", when contemplating the horrors that death might bring. Now, the suggestion maybe that by refusing to act he is anyway 'sleeping' his life away by refusing to engage with it. The rhyming couplet here carries the force of his decision – "From this time forth/My thoughts be bloody, or be nothing worth!" – and propel Hamlet back to confront Claudius.

ACT 4 SCENE 5

PLOT SUMMARY:

We open with Gertrude saying she won't "speak with her" – but don't yet know who she means. A "Gentleman" describes the waiting woman as desperate, and mad – she can't speak anything of sense and he isn't sure that she thinks anything rational at all. Horatio advises Gertrude to speak with her, and Gertrude agrees. Ophelia enters, and sings songs that seem to mean nothing. Yet her songs *are* meaningful. She sings about Polonius' death, and a maid's lost honour. Claudius and Gertrude watch her, not knowing what to say or how to react.

After Ophelia has gone, Claudius instructs Horatio to keep watch over. He tells Gertrude that this must have been caused by her father's death. He also tells her that Laertes has returned, but will not speak to anyone. He's heard rumours that as Laertes has passed through the city the people have called for him to become king.

Laertes arrives into the room, angry and accusatory. He seems to think Claudius has murdered his father, but asks what has happened and why the funeral was so swift. Claudius tells him that he was not responsible for Polonius' death, and then Ophelia enters. Laertes immediately realises that she is mad, and is grief-stricken. Ophelia, bearing flowers, hands them out around the court while she continues to sing. Claudius tells Laertes that he will tell him everything, and work with him to achieve "due content" for his father's death – Laertes agrees, and they leave to talk.

KEY THEMES:

Madness – Ophelia has been driven mad by what has happened.

Father/son relationships: Laertes and Polonius provide an interesting contrast to Hamlet and the King Laertes' speech is angry, direct and forceful – whereas Hamlet is often indecisive and vacillates between one decision and another.

FORM, STRUCTURE AND LANGUAGE

Ophelia's songs – The songs reveal more about Ophelia's thoughts and character than perhaps any of her "sane" speech does, as she uses references to old folk tales and fables that she half-remembers, finding new meaning in them. Her reference to the "baker's daughter" is a reference to a legend in which a beggar pleads for some bread – when the baker agrees, the daughter rebukes him. The beggar is the Saviour in disguise, and the daughter is turned into an owl as punishment. Her second song, about the maid, is more sexualised and perhaps indicates her suffering over her relationship with Hamlet: the maid gives her honour away on Valentine's day, and when he rejects her she is ruined.

Ophelia's use of prose: After her second song, Ophelia speaks in prose – just as Hamlet does when he is in a "mad episode".

KEY QUOTATIONS

Gentleman (about Ophelia)
speaks things in doubt,
That carry but half sense: her speech is nothing
Speech echoes thought; if Ophelia can't speak, she can't think – and yet some of her songs are more revealing than ever about her thoughts. They perhaps allow her to speak her mind when previously she has been silenced by honour and virtue.

Gertrude: Each toy seems prologue to some great amiss
The use of "toy" makes this seem childish and insignificant but then it's followed with something "great". This could be used to describe the play's structure – the small hints that propel the characters to devastating outcomes, including Ophelia's madness leading to her death, the ghost's instruction to the tragic ending.

Ophelia: Lord, we know what we are, but know not what we may be
Seeing Hamlet's deterioration, Ophelia is worried about her inadvertent effect on him – she didn't know the impact her rejection of him would have.

Claudius: When sorrows come, they come not single spies/ But in battalions
His martial language emphasises Claudius's thoughts, as he's concerned with the
rebellion outside his gates we don't really see. But he does seem to be genuinely
upset for Ophelia, and feel the depth of her tragedy. When considering Claudius'
actions and moral character, this is an important speech – he appears to feel
sorrow for the loss of her.

Claudius: poor Ophelia / Divided from herself and her fair judgment, / Without
the which we are pictures, or mere beasts

Laertes:

To hell, allegiance! vows, to the blackest devil!
Conscience and grace, to the profoundest pit!
I dare damnation. …
Let come what comes; only I'll be revenged
Most thoroughly for my father.

Unlike Hamlet, who's hesitated so far, Laertes is determined to seek revenge no
matter what the peril to his immortal soul. Hamlet, on the other hand, often
repeats that he must act, but in less forceful language.

CLOSE ANALYSISOP

Ophelia's second song:

To-morrow is Saint Valentine's day,
All in the morning betime,
And I a maid at your window,
To be your Valentine.
Then up he rose, and donn'd his clothes,
And dupp'd the chamber-door;
Let in the maid, that out a maid
Never departed more.

By Gis and by Saint Charity,
Alack, and fie for shame!
Young men will do't, if they come to't;
By cock, they are to blame.
Quoth she, before you tumbled me,
You promised me to wed.

Read more

*A theory that Ophelia is pregnant –
what do you think? -*
http://www.craftyscreenwriting.com/
ophelia.html

> So would I ha' done, by yonder sun,
> An thou hadst not come to my bed

Ophelia's songs are filled with imagery that show her madness because they are sexualised and lack the innocence that a young girl should have. They also hint at a further reason for her madness, that she has already lost her honour to Hamlet – an interpretation Branagh uses extensively in his film version.

The easy rhyme here belies the serious nature of the song; a maid has given her virginity to her "valentine" and thus has been ruined. The door "let in the maid, that out a maid never departed more" – she left having lost her honour in the room.

In the next one, she again sings of a betrayed maid – and blames the "young men will do'l if they come to't", almost tormenting herself with the thought that she has, as Polonius warned, tendered herself too cheaply. The girl in the song believes a promise of marriage, and Ophelia has earlier in the play hinted at something similar before being told sternly that Hamlet is not in her league, and unable to marry who he wants. If we believe that Hamlet has seduced and abandoned Ophelia, then her madness is also a tragic response to the realisation that she is abandoned, heartbroken and ruined.

Ophelia:

> There's rosemary, that's for remembrance; pray,
> love, remember: and there is pansies. that's for thoughts.
> …
> There's fennel for you, and columbines: there's rue
> for you; and here's some for me: we may call it
> herb-grace o' Sundays: O you must wear your rue with a difference.
> There's a daisy: I would give you
> some violets, but they withered all when my father
> died: they say he made a good end,--

As Ophelia comes into the court chamber, she hands out flowers with symbolic meanings (up until the Victorian era, giving flowers was often seen as a coded message). Having her give these to different characters heightens their meaning – rosemary and pansies to Laertes.

Fennel and columbine – flattery and deception

Rue – bitterness

Daisy – innocence

Violets – fidelity

ACT 4 SCENE 6

PLOT SUMMARY:

Sailors arrive with letters for Horatio. They're from Hamlet, telling him what has happened on board the ship to England. He reads the letter aloud: Hamlet's ship was captured by pirates, and they are returning him to Denmark, where he intends to reward them for their help. Hamlet has sent letters to the king, and Rosencrantz and Guildenstern are still on their way to England.

FORM, STRUCTURE AND LANGUAGE

Plot development – this short scene is entirely plot development, solving the tricky problem of how to get Hamlet back to Denmark!! We don't see anything of the pirate battle – partly because it's really a deus ex machina, or plot device to get Hamlet back to court, and perhaps partly because it would be expensive and difficult to stage such a different and difficult scene – not least because every other setting is "a room in the castle"! Very practical reasons mean we don't need to see the piratical battle, and in an already lengthy play, that scene is unnecessary.

ACT 4 SCENE 7

PLOT SUMMARY:

Claudius has told Laertes that Hamlet killed Polonius. When asked why he didn't say earlier, Claudius says he didn't want to hurt Gertrude, and Hamlet is so beloved by the public that he wasn't sure they would accept it. Laertes blames Hamlet for both his father's death and his sister's madness, and swears revenge. Claudius receives Hamlet's letter and reads it privately – it tells him Hamlet is returned, and will come the next day to explain himself. Laertes hears Claudius' confusion and comes back.

Claudius leads Laertes in constructing a plan for revenge that will seem like an accident: even Gertrude will think so. Laertes is famed as a great swordsman and Hamlet has, since hearing that report, wanted to have a chance to fight Laertes to test himself. Claudius, provoking and manipulating Laertes, challenges him and asks if he is genuinely serious about avenging his father, no matter what. When Laertes replies that he will do anything (see Close Analysis), Claudius tells him to challenge Hamlet. Laertes adds that he will dip his sword in poison so that whenever Hamlet is scratched with it, he will be fatally wounded.

Gertrude interrupts the two of them to tell them that Ophelia has been found, drowned in the river. Laertes seems not to believe her at first, repeating "drowned", but then leaves in grief. Claudius tells Gertrude that he has calmed Laertes, but fears that this will re-invigorate his anger.

KEY THEMES:

Fathers and sons – Laertes is the foil to Hamlet and here his desire to seek vengeance is a counterpart to Hamlet's inaction.

Revenge – Laertes says he will kill Hamlet in the chapel if need be – the very place that Hamlet could not kill Claudius.

FORM, STRUCTURE AND LANGUAGE

Doubling of Laertes and Hamlet – Laertes' actions, including his willingness to avenge his father by committing murder, is a counterpart or foil to Hamlet – the difference between them exacerbates the contrast and makes us question Hamlet's choices.

CONTEXT:

The word suicide isn't associated with Ophelia's drowning. Gertrude says she "fell" into the river. Suicide is a mortal sin, as Hamlet has said in the first soliloquy, and therefore Ophelia will be denied entry to heaven in the after-life. Keeping the true nature of her death secret would be essential to her remaining honour.

KEY QUOTATIONS

Claudius:
The queen his mother
Lives almost by his looks; and for myself--
My virtue or my plague, be it either which--
She's so conjunctive to my life and soul,
That, as the star moves not but in his sphere,
I could not but by her.
Claudius' love for Gertrude is "my virtue or my plague", the two opposites perhaps indicating the conflict he feels. He recognises that Hamlet is the central point of Gertrude's life, the "star" will not move if he is not around. Yet Claudius is also rather poetic here – "so conjunctive to my life and soul...I could not but by her" – implying that he genuinely does love Gertrude. However, as ever,

consider whether here he's simply manipulating Laertes with a romantic reason why he has not dealt with Hamlet already.

Claudius:
for his death no wind of blame shall breathe,
But even his mother shall uncharge the practise
And call it accident.

Here, Claudius isn't so romantic! The plot means even Gertrude will see it as an accident. "No wind of blame shall breathe", and the two of them will be able to get away with murder – again.

CLOSE ANALYSIS

Claudius:
Laertes, was your father dear to you?
Or are you like the painting of a sorrow,
A face without a heart?

Not that I think you did not love your father;
But that I know love is begun by time;
And that I see, in passages of proof,
Time qualifies the spark and fire of it.
There lives within the very flame of love
A kind of wick or snuff that will abate it;
And nothing is at a like goodness still;
For goodness, growing to a plurisy,
Dies in his own too much: that we would do
We should do when we would; for this 'would' changes
And hath abatements and delays as many
As there are tongues, are hands, are accidents;
And then this 'should' is like a spendthrift sigh,
That hurts by easing. But, to the quick o' the ulcer:--
Hamlet comes back: what would you undertake,
To show yourself your father's son in deed
More than in words?

Claudius insults Laertes as part of his manipulation while convincing him to challenge Hamlet. He questions his grief – a contrast to the beginning when he told Hamlet his grief was "unmanly" for continuing so long. Now he uses grief as a symbol of Laertes's love for his father to propel him into the fight. He accepts that grief, and love, wanes with time – "time disqualifies the spark" – and perhaps Laertes has come to accept his father's death. Yet from what we know of Claudius this seems most likely a ruse to prick Laertes' conscience and pride, and force him into action.

LAERTES

To cut his throat i' the church.

KING CLAUDIUS

No place, indeed, should murder sanctuarize;
Revenge should have no bounds. But, good Laertes,
Will you do this, keep close within your chamber.
Hamlet return'd shall know you are come home:

When Laertes replies "I'd cut his throat i' the chapel," it's a reminder of what Hamlet couldn't do – once again Laertes acts as a foil or counterpart to Hamlet, drawing attention to the fact that he couldn't or wouldn't act. For Laertes, it seems the need to end Hamlet's life is more important than *when*. He doesn't consider ensuring that his soul goes to hell. Does this suggest Laertes is more interested in justice than vengeance? Yet Claudius takes this as meaning that Laertes is interested in revenge – but then, he doesn't know how close he came to death in the earlier chapel.

Gertrude

There is a willow grows aslant a brook,
That shows his hoar leaves in the glassy stream;
There with fantastic garlands did she come
Of crow-flowers, nettles, daisies, and long purples
That liberal shepherds give a grosser name,
But our cold maids do dead men's fingers call them:
There, on the pendent boughs her coronet weeds
Clambering to hang, an envious sliver broke;
When down her weedy trophies and herself
Fell in the weeping brook. Her clothes spread wide;

Gertrude's description of Ophelia again links her with nature and flowers; the willow weeps into the brook, hanging over it and is a symbol of grief. The "long purples" are known as "dead men's fingers" – another macabre image associated with her death.

Gertrude's language here is perhaps startlingly poetic with its descriptive language and long, meandering sentences; it's her longest speech and memorialises Ophelia as beautiful, one with nature, almost ethereal in her death. Ophelia crowns herself – a strange action but if we believe she's been abandoned by Hamlet, perhaps her madness leads her to enact a successful coronation?

And, mermaid-like, awhile they bore her up:
Which time she chanted snatches of old tunes;
As one incapable of her own distress,
Or like a creature native and indued
Unto that element: but long it could not be
Till that her garments, heavy with their drink,
Pull'd the poor wretch from her melodious lay
To muddy death.

Placing "fell" on the beginning of the line draws attention to the lie Gertrude tells – Ophelia is later explained as committing suicide. By returning Ophelia to water, "mermaid like", Shakespeare makes her tragedy almost other-worldly, and it is this scene that painters have recreated time and time again.

ACT 5 SCENE 1

PLOT SUMMARY:

In a churchyard, two "clowns" – gravediggers, in fact – are digging Ophelia's grave and grumbling about the fact that she is going to be given a Christian burial despite her suicide; a class criticism as they point out that if she wasn't a high-born lady, she wouldn't have been given a Christian funeral. The gravedigger sings as he digs. Hamlet, coming across the scene, is appalled at the apparent lack of feeling. He then starts throwing a skull (juggling it perhaps) and Hamlet comments to Horatio that the skull used to be a person, but it's impossible to tell who it might have been – implying that we're all the same after death.

Hamlet speaks to the digger to ask whose grave it will be. The digger replies a woman's. When asked how long he's been a gravedigger, he replies since King Hamlet overcame Fortinbras, and before the young Hamlet went mad and was sent to England – clearly unaware he's speaking to the young Hamlet. The other gravedigger has been there longer, and tells Hamlet that if a corpse is not "rotten before he dies" then he'll last eight or nine years before fully rotting in the ground. He shows Hamlet a skull that has been there twenty-three years, a man named Yorick, the King's jester. Hamlet remarks that he knew Yorick and remembers his laughter and songs, but they are all gone now. Hamlet and Horatio muse once more that, after death, all men are the same.

They're interrupted by the arrival of the court, including the King, Queen and Laertes, come to bury Ophelia – as Hamlet discovers when Laertes refers to his sister. Laertes, grief-stricken, leaps into the grave as Gertrude strews flowers in it. Hamlet, too, jumps in and when Laertes sees him, he attacks and they fight. When they're pulled out, Hamlet says he loved Ophelia, and in a confused, rapid series of rhetorical questions, expresses his confusion and grief over her death in his absence. He leaves the scene abruptly. Claudius goes to Laertes and tells him to have patience, and assures Gertrude that they will deal with Hamlet shortly.

KEY THEMES:

Religion – Ophelia shouldn't be buried in a graveyard (suicides weren't allowed burial on hallowed ground) but because she's high-born, the rules can be bent for her.

FORM, STRUCTURE AND LANGUAGE

The gravediggers – although some of their comedy and word play has become dated, or even lost, the comic interruption of the gravediggers comes at a crucial moment. Everything is about to come to a head: Hamlet is confronting Claudius, Claudius and Laertes have a plan, and Ophelia is dead – but Hamlet doesn't yet know. By pausing for a moment in this comic interlude, Shakespeare heightens the tension and makes us want to return to the main storyline. He also uses it as a moment (ironically) of light relief, before the final events of the last scenes. They also serve a vital function in dramatically telling Hamlet of Ophelia's death and propelling him into the final battle.

CONTEXT:

Religion – Ophelia should have been buried in unconsecrated ground, as a suicide, but Claudius' orders – and money – have bought her a grave.

KEY QUOTATIONS

Gravedigger: If this had not been a gentlewoman, she should have been buried out o' Christian burial.

Hamlet:
That skull had a tongue in it, and could sing once:
how the knave jowls it to the ground, as if it were

Cain's jaw-bone, that did the first murder! It
might be the pate of a politician, which this ass
now o'er-reaches

Through the scene Hamlet refers to several possible owners of the skull, from
Cain and a politician, to lawyer, courtier or a landowner – the suggestion is that
the skull could have been anyone and, with all the extras of life stripped away
from them, they are simply the same after all.

Priest:
her death was doubtful;
And, but that great command o'ersways the order,
She should in ground unsanctified have lodged
Till the last trumpet

The priest implies that Claudius – the "great command" – has overruled the
Church's command that suicides not be buried in church grounds. It implies that
Claudius is over-stepping his earthly boundaries to interfere with religious
matters, although of course the priest has complied. This could be a criticism of
religion – that their stance is unreasonable and *should* be overruled – or it might
be a criticism of Claudius attempting to influence the church and therefore
exposing his lack of genuine religious belief.

Hamlet:
I loved Ophelia: forty thousand brothers
Could not, with all their quantity of love,
Make up my sum.

Simple, straightforward language again – the heartbroken declaration "I loved
Ophelia" with the caesura, pausing before he compares his love with Laertes' for
his sister.

Hamlet:
Be buried quick with her, and so will I:

ACT 5 SCENE 2

PLOT SUMMARY:

Horatio and Hamlet appear onstage; Hamlet tells Horatio that he read a letter
from Claudius telling England to murder him. On reading it, Hamlet instead
rewrote a letter, asking England to kill immediately those who are carrying the
letter – Rosencrantz and Guildenstern. This ensures that the two will be killed

straight away, without "shriving time", the prayer that would cleanse their souls: Hamlet has arranged for these two what he could not do with his uncle in the chapel. Hamlet is adamant that he will seek revenge on Claudius, but admits that he regrets attacking Laertes, whose grief is equal to his own.

Osric, a messenger, arrives and speaks highly of Laertes' skill with a sword. He tells Hamlet that Claudius has placed a bet on the two of them fighting, and Hamlet winning. Hamlet sees there is something happening, but agrees to the fight and sends Osric back to accept it. Horatio warns him against it but Hamlet insists that he will continue anyway.

Beginning the fight in front of the court, Hamlet apologises for any wrong done to Laertes, who accepts, and says he will not seek vengeance, but honour must still be satisfied and so they must continue. Hamlet praises Laertes' skill "like a star i' the darkest night", and says he looks forward to a friendly duel.

To Osric, Claudius says he must have a glass of wine so that if Hamlet looks as though he's winning, the king can drink to his health and fortune. He'll also poison Hamlet's glass so that when he joins the toast, he'll die.

Although the duel reaches that point, Hamlet says he doesn't need a drink yet and they continue. Gertrude picks up the poisoned wine and drinks from it instead – Claudius can't stop her without revealing himself. Through the course of the duel, Laertes seems to be having second thoughts and, in an aside, says it's "against my conscience". He wounds Hamlet; they drop their rapiers and then Hamlet picks up the poisoned blade, and stabs Laertes.

Gertrude falls to the floor – they think at first she's fainted at Hamlet's injury but she realises she has been poisoned, and then dies. Laertes admits that he has poisoned Hamlet with the rapier, and that the King has been a part of the entire plot. Hamlet then stabs Claudius, poisoning him with the blade. He then forces Claudius to drink the remains of the poisoned wine, and Claudius dies.

Laertes has enough time to ask Hamlet's forgiveness, and to forgive him for his own and Polonius' death. Then he dies. Even with his last breaths, Hamlet is blaming Gertrude – "wretched queen, adieu!". He then speaks to Horatio, asking him to "report me and my cause aright", to let everyone know the truth of what has happened. he also says that Fortinbras "has my dying voice", essentially naming him as the heir to Denmark. Then Hamlet, too, dies.

Horatio is the last one alive onstage when Fortinbras arrives, and asks what has happened. Horatio says he will explain all, truthfully and honestly. He also tells Fortinbras that he is the next king of Denmark.

KEY THEMES:

Honour or vengeance? At the beginning of the fight, Laertes says he won't seek vengeance but honour must be satisfied.

Death – virtually everyone dies! Horatio and Fortinbras alone are left: the only two wholly good characters?

FORM, STRUCTURE AND LANGUAGE

Revenge tragedy – the typical bloodbath ending comes to pass here; everybody dies – including Claudius for two reasons, just to be sure. Hamlet is given a final voice, enabling him to ask that his story is repeated faithfully. The ending, with Fortinbras' speech, implies that here, finally, is a ruler who is fit to lead after all.

Hamlet will live on: In Horatio's comments that the story and memory of Hamlet will continue to be told, is Shakespeare alluding to his own hopes for the play?

The ending: Fortinbras becomes ruler of Denmark. Order is restored, out of the chaos of the natural order created by Claudius' murder of his brother. By giving Hamlet the full funeral rites and honours of a solider, the honour of Fortinbras is also established to confirm that Denmark now will rise again.

KEY QUOTATIONS

Hamlet: They are not near my conscience; their defeat
Does by their own insinuation grow:
'Tis dangerous when the baser nature comes
Between the pass and fell incensed points
Of mighty opposites.
The deaths of Rosencrantz and Guildenstern don't concern Hamlet. Is this an indictment of the treatment of ordinary people? Shakespeare's language here suggests that when two "mighty opposites" fight, those in the middle are the ones who pay the price. But it also includes the suggestion that their "baser natures" are what have caused them to choose a side, and therefore they have died as a result. Their "own insinuation" has caused their defeat, and Hamlet refuses to feel guilty for their deaths, despite Horatio's disapproval.

Hamlet: He that hath kill'd my king and whored my mother,
Very blunt and aggressive language but here, at least, Hamlet, using the active verb, seems to be entirely blaming Claudius for his actions rather than Gertrude.

Horatio: If your mind dislike any thing, obey it:
A wise aphorism from Horatio, warning Hamlet - Horatio remains honest and loyal to the last moment, and here touches on a core principle of the play: perhaps Hamlet's inability to kill Claudius earlier is in fact because murder is wrong, no matter what the justification?

Laertes: I am satisfied in nature,
Whose motive, in this case, should stir me most
To my revenge: but in my terms of honour
I stand aloof; and will no reconcilement
The conflict between revenge and honour is an important one and sometimes frustrating to a modern audience – here, Laertes sees that vengeance is not required, but there is still a question of justice to consider.

Claudius: Gertrude, do not drink.
Gertrude: I will, my lord; I pray you, pardon me.
Claudius: [Aside] It is the poison'd cup: it is too late.
Claudius' aside *could* be quite desperate if we believe he loves Gertrude. Or is he afraid that the poison killing her will reveal him too soon? Her last words to Claudius are "pardon me" – does she have a double meaning here? Is there any possibility that she knows the wine is poisoned and that she is saving Hamlet's life?

Laertes: the king, the king's to blame.
Repetition for emphasis, and the final out-loud acknowledgement that Claudius is to blame, not only for this final situation but an audience can agree that "the king" is to blame for the earlier tragedy as well that has brought us here.

Hamlet: Here, thou incestuous, murderous, damned Dane,
Drink off this potion
The violent aggressive language here encapsulating what Claudius has been responsible for – incestuous, murderous – and the "damned" nature of his punishment as well, being damned for eternity, remembering of course that Hamlet didn't kill him in the chapel because he thought he was praying and 'clean'). Once again, Hamlet puts the sexual transgression first; **incestuous**, murderous.

Horatio: Now cracks a noble heart. Good night sweet prince:
And flights of angels sing thee to thy rest!
Horatio's grief at Hamlet's death reminds us how loyal he has been throughout, but is he a little misguided – at all? – to suggest that angels should accompany Hamlet, who has just murdered two people?

Fortinbras: Bear Hamlet, like a soldier, to the stage;
For he was likely, had he been put on,
To have proved most royally: and, for his passage,
The soldiers' music and the rites of war
Speak loudly for him.
The final lines onstage are given to Fortinbras, the new likely ruler of Denmark. He immediately honours Hamlet, giving him an honour guard for a funeral, the "rites of war" and "soldier's music" to celebrate his previous rival. This indicates a restoration of true honour to Denmark, a leader who celebrates the strengths of the vanquished. He is also generous, acknowledging that Hamlet would "have proved most royally" and been a good king, given the chance. Order is restored, with Fortinbras on the throne – the resolution to the revenge tragedy.

CONTEXT

THE SUCCESSION QUESTION

Elizabethan England was concerned with what would happen when the Queen died – there's some complicated political details about the succession, and who would inherit the throne. And there's a huge problem in *talking* about it, because in 1586 Elizabeth made it an act of treason to discuss who would follow her.

Essentially, nobody could agree who would be next. Elizabeth remained unmarried and childless – so no obvious successor. Her cousin, Mary Queen of Scots, should probably have been next but Elizabeth's father had written a clause in his will saying her family should never inherit, and there was another law that said anyone "outside the allegiance of England" wouldn't inherit – which really was aimed at Mary. She was also foreign, and a Catholic – two things very few people wanted in an English ruler. Eventually, Elizabeth had her found guilty of treason and beheaded. There were several other contenders – eventually, it came down to James Stuart (Mary's son) – he managed to take the throne *partly* as the best connected, and *partly* because he made friends with the right influential people in Elizabeth's court prior to her death. He became James I of England, and James VI of Scotland.

How to apply this:

Don't info-dump the politics! All that above really means is: there was no clear successor, and everyone was worried. It's really destabilising to not have anyone in charge, and potentially leads to years of conflict as dukes and lords fight it out to see who can take the throne.

We might find it odd that Claudius, King Hamlet's brother, takes the throne – Elizabethans would have seen this as old-fashioned or archaic, but not unfamiliar. And because Claudius has no children, the throne would then eventually pass back to Hamlet – unless of course perhaps he and Gertrude had children (it's not clear how old Gertrude is – do you think this is a possibility?) Being forbidden to murder a king and then take his throne is clearly applicable and Claudius' revolution is relatively bloodless with only one death: the king's. The question of succession isn't uncommon in Shakespeare. In *Macbeth* (written when James was on the throne), Shakespeare explores the hereditary nature of the throne – Macbeth and Banquo both want their sons to be king. In *Hamlet,*

Claudius doesn't seem concerned about his children continuing the family line. His power is all for himself.

THE ROLES AND EXPECTATIONS OF WOMEN

Read more

Always a complex thing, this! It's easy to think "olden days: women had a terrible time." But that, clearly, is far too simple for an A-Level student's thinking! And it certainly wasn't all bad in the Elizabethan era. No, women couldn't vote or be in politics, or have any number of public offices but when we're talking about *roles of women*, a lot of the time –

The RSC have a great summary of some more unusual elements of performance - https://www.rsc.org.uk/Hamlet/about-the-play/stage-history

and particularly with *Hamlet* – we're talking about *gentlewomen*. Women of high social status, not the women who've always had to work in the home and at a range of jobs to keep their families fed and housed. They didn't have a particularly great time but then neither, often, did working class men. In *Hamlet*, we're dealing with the very top of the social ladder: royalty. So there are conventions and expectations, particularly regarding honour, virginity and status related to their families. But there's also Elizabeth on the throne and, while she had male advisors, she was very clear that she was in charge no matter what her gender. She gave a speech at Tilbury[1] which made this plain: **"I know I have the body of a weak, feeble woman; but I have the heart and stomach of a king, and of a king of England too"**

How to apply this:

Neither Gertrude nor Ophelia is Elizabeth – they don't have the same authority she has and they're dependent on the men around them in different ways. Where they're most vulnerable is their honour, and that's determined by their gender. The expectations were not only of virginity before marriage, but women were supposed to be submissive, and not enjoy sex. Widows who were financially solvent, such as Gertrude, weren't really expected to remarry and, as Hamlet says, that Gertrude does is taken of evidence that she has an unnaturally voracious sexual appetite. When Ophelia goes mad, her songs are filled with sexual references and it's these shocking verses that are what most critics, and characters, think are evidence of her madness – no noble woman would ever say

---

[1] Where troops were waiting to repel the Spanish Armada sailing round the coast of England.

74

such things. Which perhaps begs the question: how does Ophelia know them in the first place?

STAGECRAFT AT THE GLOBE, LONDON

The first performance of *Hamlet* was at the Globe. Many performances took place mid-afternoon – obviously no stage lighting! Although *Hamlet's* set in the 13th century, it was performed in Elizabethan contemporary costume. There would have been props and minimal staging, and, of course, a trapdoor.

How to apply this:

Think about the provenance, or origins, of the play. The ghost – the central opening figure – doesn't appear at midnight at all, or in some darkened battlement. It's broad daylight, in a crowd of hundreds of people all busy, talking and not necessarily *immediately* paying attention. The audience has to suspend their disbelief – no matter *how* fervently they believe in ghosts! The trap-door's also specifically referenced when the ghost is "below", and we hear the off-stage voice from beneath the stage.

RELIGION

Elizabethan England was Protestant – one of the reasons for the succession issues (above) was that Mary Queen of Scots was Catholic. There was a conflict between different ways of worshipping – who could speak directly to God and who had to go through a priest, the ceremony and rituals more common in Catholicism, and so on. However, *Hamlet* also has some deeper religious connotations.

How to apply this:

Claudius makes his soldiers work on Sundays – as stated right at the beginning - which makes him irreligious, ignoring the Sabbath and making others ignore it too.

Whether the ghost comes from heaven, hell or purgatory perhaps affects how we view it and its truthfulness – there's plenty of evidence for heaven and hell, so it's difficult to decide. The concept of religion and punishment is also important; Hamlet doesn't kill Claudius when he thinks he's prayed for forgiveness, so that Claudius won't be permitted direct entry to heaven. Without confessing immediately before death, Claudius would be sent to hell – as Rosencrantz and Guildenstern are, and the old King.

Wittenberg, Hamlet's university, is referenced only briefly but it is potentially significant – it's the place where Martin Luther sparked the Protestant Reformation by essentially criticising the Catholic Church for corruption, and insisting on a more personal relationship with God, including not having to speak through priests, and being able to read the Bible in one's own language instead of Latin. While it's only a quick mention, the fact Hamlet is studying at Wittenberg (although, in the setting of the play, significantly before Martin Luther) symbolises his role as a thoughtful, intelligent and intellectual young man – but perhaps also rather impetuous.

ATTITUDES TOWARDS SUICIDE

The Church excommunicated people who committed suicide – they could not be buried in consecrated /holy ground (churchyards) and they would not be able to pass into heaven. This is referenced in Hamlet's first soliloquy, and Ophelia's death is presumed suicide – hence the conversation between the gravediggers about the injustice of her burial. Ophelia can be buried there because Claudius has intervened with a combination of power and money, probably, and bought an indulgence or similar from the church so that she can have a Christian burial.

TRAVELLING PLAYERS

The first theatre in London was built when Shakespeare was a boy; before that, groups of players frequently toured the country and performed wherever they could find a local space, often churches or other community buildings. With the development of professional theatres, players could set up and perform permanently. Shakespeare's company worked at one of these, with a patron who could pay for the theatre and fund the company. For those who didn't have the patrons to buy a theatre, they continued to travel the country. The travelling companies were often the starting point for actors, who worked their way to a permanent job in a developing city.

How to apply this:

Travelling players were often distrusted – mainly because they were transient, didn't stay long, and were easy targets so developed a reputation for being thieves or deceptive. The actors in *Hamlet* are clearly willing to do what it takes to get their play onstage – including adding in the additional speech that Hamlet writes for them. Hamlet manipulates the players partly because they are a separate group, who won't be there for long and are detached from the events at court, and in the rest of Denmark. Doing this means that he's aligning himself with a slightly unknown group, but is using them to get what he wants – and he doesn't have anybody around him that he can trust (other than Horatio)..

USING CRITICAL VIEWS AND INTERPRETATION

For AO5 – alternative views – there are two strands on the mark-scheme:

- Judgement consistently informed by exploration of different interpretations of the text
- Judgement consistently informed by changing critical views of the text over time.

This means that you need to be able to explore a range of different interpretations, and that *some* of those interpretations need to be a **critical view**. This either means viewing it through a critical lens, such as feminism or Marxism, or could be using a specifically named critic. *You don't have to memorise lots of critics' quotations.* Paraphrasing is acceptable, and you don't have to use named critics - the broader schools of criticism are also acceptable.

USING A CRITICAL VIEWPOINT

Think of the phrase "looking through rose-tinted glasses". Everything appears pink; we know the phrase means everything *seems* happy, almost perfect. Looking at a text through a critical viewpoint is the same in some ways; it's coloured by that lens, and everything in it is somehow informed by that understanding. So for example looking at texts in a feminist way aims to explore the ways that the texts are shaped by their creation within a patriarchal system: how far do they reflect or challenge, support or expose it?

This is part of the interplay of writer and audience – the writer may have certain ideas in mind, but the audience has a different experience to them. Does that make their interpretation less valid, because the writer didn't see it at the time? The interpretation absolutely has to **make sense** – but writers, like anyone else, have a huge wealth of experiences and beliefs, and sometimes are influenced by ideas they're not consciously thinking about. A writer might not set out to write a play about the political unrest of the time, but because that's the time they are in, it leaks through into the way characters speak and behave.

There are lots of different critical theories – and thousands of critics on *Hamlet*! I've chosen a few viewpoints I think are the most useful for this level, and this specification, and some critics I think are interesting. Hopefully you'll also do some further independent reading and come up with some of your own.

SCHOOLS OF CRITICAL THEORY

it's important when you're using these theories not to apply an anachronistic label – Shakespeare can't **be a Marxist** because Marxism came a long time **after** him. BUT you can say "A Marxist interpretation suggests, " or "the proto- [before] feminist representation of Gertrude," etc.

FEMINISM: To explore the ways a text is affected by the patriarchal society in which it was created. How does it reflect or challenge the position of women in society? How are female characters and experiences being presented?

How to apply this:

Shakespeare as a feminist? This view interprets Gertrude as a powerful woman. She's a widow – which gives her unusual power as a widow, having control over herself and having had the sexual experience men might find threatening. By marrying Claudius – her own choice now – she maintains authority and power in a royal court where she'd quickly become irrelevant. In the relationship with Claudius, it's not always clear who's in control – there's some suggestion they're very in love, some that it's a marriage of power and circumstance – with her, he's more likely to be accepted by the rest of the court. She manipulates those around her, including Hamlet and Claudius. Is this a feminist character, who can take control of her own destiny, or a criticism of the inherent manipulative deception of women?

Shakespeare criticising women? In addition to the potential criticism above, Gertrude's sexuality is severely criticised many times – and she is sometimes defined by her sexuality rather than any other attributes. Is Shakespeare suggesting all she has to contribute is sex? Hamlet's slurs are almost always about her sexual appetite – are we supposed to agree with him, or think that because he is mad, he's mistreating her?

See also the changing feminist viewpoints below.

MARXISM: A Marxist interpretation sees texts as a political struggle reflective of their society. Karl Marx identified two sections of society, the bourgeoisie (the dominant class, owners of land and wealth) and the proletariat (subordinate, participating in production/the economy but not owning or controlling it). History is a struggle between these two classes. Marx famously wrote "religion is the opiate of the masses" – Marxism often sees society as putting the proletariat in their place and pacifying them into believing that's where they should be, rising the bourgeoisie up. In literary terms, we look at the politics of a text – who is in

78

control and how this is exerted, where the power comes from. There's also a discussion about whether a text is itself a tool of control – does the proletariat stay happy and content because of the literature the bourgeoisie produce for them?

How to apply this:

This is a play about politics, succession and power. The powerful characters are unpleasant, cruel – murderous, even – a savage critique of the bourgeoisie. Is Shakespeare criticising the court by portraying the squabbling, infighting and destructive natures of those in power? On the other hand, he does introduce Fortinbras as a strong, noble hero – so is it about the right *kind* of power? If so, that contributes more to the Marxist interpretation that Shakespeare is propping up the bourgeoisie by lulling the proletariat (the audience at the Globe?) into accepting that there is a right kind of power – so implicitly accepting the power and control of another class.

NEW HISTORICISM: Often applied to Shakespeare, and embedded into our exam system! This looks at writers as reflections of their time and argues that we need to understand their social, historical and cultural contexts in order to understand their work – and conversely we can also understand more about the concerns of their time by reading the work. For Shakespeare, we need to consider the Tudor political situation, the religious struggles of the previous decades, the expectations of Renaissance women – and we can understand what Renaissance English considered important, or thought about important themes, through the way they're treated in *Hamlet*.

How to apply this:

- **Concerns about the succession following Elizabeth I**
- **Roles and expectations of women, particularly noble-born women of the time**
  Gertrude subverts the expectations of women by quickly remarrying – Hamlet's sexualized slurs are in part because she is expressing, through her actions, a sexuality that makes him uncomfortable. Ophelia, on the other hand, is obedient to all the men around her and is clearly acquiescent when her father tells her to reject Hamlet.
- **Considerations of madness**
  Madness was thought to be "internalization of disobedience" – so Hamlet's madness is a result of his refusal to obey his father's wishes.
- **Religious beliefs**

Another critical conflict in Elizabethan England; following Elizabeth's accession, Catholics (previously promoted under her sister Mary's reign) were 'strongly encouraged' to convert to Protestantism, which – unlike Catholicism – doesn't include Purgatory. The ghost may be from Purgatory, however, suggesting a debate between the two doctrines.

PSYCHOANALYTICAL: Exploring the ways texts are representative of the conscious and the subconscious, particularly influenced by the works of Sigmund Freud.

Although a Psychology student would have more detail on Freud – I hope! – in terms of literary theory, the key points are these:

- People are deeply confused and concerned about sex, and this manifests itself in a range of different ways.
- The classic "Oedipus complex" (named for the character in the Greek play where this happens) is that in growing up, the role model idea becomes a little too literal. The son wants to take his father's place, which involves killing his father and sleeping with his mother. (The converse is the Electra complex, for women wanting to replace their mothers).

How to apply this:

Therefore, Hamlet's frustration and anger with Gertrude is potentially misdirected – rather than being angry with her for betraying his father and marrying his uncle, he's actually angrier that Claudius has managed to achieve what he has been unable to do – take his father's place. When he's raging at Gertrude's sexuality, he's also angry with himself for his subconscious desires.

His inability to act – say, for example kill Claudius in the chapel – could be because he sees himself in Claudius, and subconsciously admires his actions.

SPECIFIC CRITICAL INTERPRETATIONS

Remember that when you're using critical interpretation, it has to be linked very carefully to the text – don't suddenly dump all this learned information into your essay! For example, an essay on indecision could use the conflict between early and Romantic interpretations. One on trust might use the changing feminist viewpoint and link it to the breakdown of trust between Hamlet and Gertrude as a reaction to her sexuality.

PASSION VS. REASON: HAMLET'S DELAY IN KILLING CLAUDIUS

Early criticism (late 1600s) criticised the play for being too passionate, too angry, violent and emotional – the Puritans closed the theatres because they wanted to encourage movement away from this very expressive art to a more serious, considered way of life. The sexual and religious immorality of the play meant that Hamlet's delay is because he's *too* passionate – the quiet lonely death in the chapel isn't enough for him: he wants blood.

Romantic poets (early-mid 1800s), including Coleridge and Keats, saw Hamlet as intellectually curious, too sensitive and tending to melancholy – personality traits that fascinated the Romantic movement which prized sensation and experience over everything else. They also saw this intense emotional intellectual quality as setting Hamlet above everyone around him, therefore meaning he's the only one who sees the situation for what it is

This debate is particularly relevant for Hamlet's delay in killing Claudius despite his opportunity; for Romantics, he pauses because he is too intellectual – reasoned – and thinks too much about the consequences. William Hazlitt, also a Romantic, said that Hamlet is the "most amiable of misanthropes".

A.C. Bradley, in the early 20th century, argued instead that Hamlet's delay was because he was unable to cope with being in the position that he's in. His lack of action is caused because in truth he blames Gertrude more than Claudius, and cannot reconcile or decide who is most deserving of vengeance.

C.S. Lewis, in the mid-1900s, said it didn't matter. *Hamlet* is about an exploration of human tragedy and behaviour – Hamlet's reasons at that moment aren't explained by Shakespeare – the mystery of why he hesitates is part of the drama.

FEMINIST CHANGES

17th century – Jeremy Collier, among others, criticised the portrayal of Ophelia's madness, writing that making her immodest was unnecessary and further diminished her character.

Ophelia's portrayal could represent a critique of the double standards of Elizabethan expectations of women. Polonius and Laertes both criticise her for having a relationship with Hamlet, but Laertes seems able to behave as he wishes. Laertes is told to trust his judgement, but Ophelia is commanded by her father.

Late 20th century – Elaine Showalter explores madness as related to control, or the lack of it. She argues that madness is caused by an inability to control one's life, and "hysterical" is a term applied to women who exhibit more unusual behaviours – not a medical condition but a social label of control. In Ophelia's case, her madness is caused by her inability to balance her own desires with the wishes of her father, brother and Hamlet. Some critics also argue that madness is used to give women a voice that they wouldn't have otherwise.

Ophelia is merely a cipher – she's there purely to give Hamlet something to react against, rather than being developed as a character in her own right, therefore Shakespeare is reflective of the misogynist attitudes of his time – women only being important for what they represent or show about men.

20th century discussion of Gertrude focuses on whether she's a victim or not as well. Can we believe the sexual slurs of Hamlet - and how far does it matter? Is Gertrude naïve and unaware of Claudius' involvement in her husband's death? She may be more powerful than she appears. Whether she knew about the murder plot or not, following the death of old Hamlet she loses any influence she may have had over the kingdom, which she only gained through marriage. However, by marrying Claudius she potentially regains that authority and position. She also potentially has married to satisfy a sexual appetite – but again, ideas over time have changed as to whether this is a terrible action or understandable.

OTHER CRITICS

Samuel Johnson 1765 – parts of the play are "Too horrible to be read or uttered", and Hamlet's treatment of Ophelia is unnecessarily cruel. "Hamlet is, through the whole play, rather an instrument than an agent"

Coleridge (1818) – Shakespeare is highlighting the necessity for "an equilibrium between the real and the imaginary worlds"

A. C. Swinburne (1880): "it should be plain to any reader that the signal characteristic of Hamlet's inmost nature is by no means irresolution or hesitation or any form of weakness, but rather the strong conflux of contending forces"

USING FILMS TO EXPLORE ALTERNATIVE INTERPRETATIONS

There are some absolutely superb versions of Hamlet available, and you should definitely watch several. This helps you get the plot and character, it helps fix quotes in your memory – they're associated with the context of the film, the actor's voice, and so on. You can also use the director and actors as critics – they've made the choices of how to interpret the character, and created their perspective.

The most effective way to do this is to look at the same scene in different films – do watch the whole thing but for this AO, comparison of films is most useful. For Ophelia, for example, consider the way Helena Bonham-Carter plays her madness in Mel Gibson's film, a childlike waif who seems to be the victim of sexual trauma in her post-madness interactions, compared with Kate Winslet's nineteenth-century Bedlamite, hysterical with flashbacks of sex with Hamlet and a series of brutal treatments including hydrotherapy in a straitjacket.

Compare Ophelia's argument with Hamlet. Kate Winslet's Ophelia is quiet, young, and tragic. Branagh as Hamlet looks into the mirror before she arrives – where Polonius and Claudius are hiding to watch, implying that he's already aware that she's been instructed. His kiss seems almost like a goodbye, moments before she "redelivers" his remembrances – and his denial, knowing they're watching, is because he feels betrayed by her.

Helena Bonham-Carter's Ophelia is walking while reading, an act designed so Gibson's Hamlet seems to come across her by chance, whereas Winslet looks directly at Branagh, intense and close, Bonham-Carter doesn't meet Gibson's eyes and doesn't move close until talking of the "sweet breath" that composed the letters, when she moves closer to him. Gibson circles her threateningly, shouting in her face while she holds her book like a shield, and he violently takes hold of her and throws her against the wall – "go to!" – which adds to his madness. Gibson's movements are often similar to those of Lawrence Olivier, circling Ophelia and shouting at her. Olivier delivers his lines with quiet intensity that makes the audience believe he cannot be mad, whereas Gibson already teeters on the brink.

The RSC version is different again – Hamlet is physically above her on the stairs as she approaches, symbolising his authority here – suggesting maybe that he's aware of the purpose behind her approach. The actor also grabs Ophelia, pulling her painfully close then throwing her down again, before wrenching at her hair – who could help but side with Ophelia here, yet Hamlet's misery is also evident.

OTHER QUOTATIONS ABOUT TRAGEDY:

While these quotes aren't specifically related to *Hamlet*, they might be useful either to frame a question or as part of a discussion about the tragic elements of *Hamlet*.

"Tragedy is more important than love. Out of all human events, it is tragedy alone that brings people out of their own petty desires and into awareness of other humans' suffering. Tragedy occurs in human lives so that we will learn to reach out and comfort others" --**C. S. Lewis**

"What makes a tragedy so tragic is not that the noble individual falls into ruin, but that his fall causes so much suffering in others." **Charmezel Dudt.**

"If a single person dies in front of you, it is a tragedy. If a million people die on the other side of the earth, it is a statistic." **(Josef Stalin is the only credit I can find for this, which seems strange perhaps but intriguing!)**

"I've never thought of my characters as being sad. On the contrary, they are full of life. They didn't choose tragedy. Tragedy chose them." --**Juliette Binoche**

"We participate in tragedy. At comedy we only look." --**Aldous Huxley**

CONSTRUCTING ALTERNATIVE VIEWPOINTS

"Alternative viewpoints" doesn't have to mean critics – you *do* need some for the second strand of AO5, but it can also be about making your own choices of interpretation. You can practice this by doing a "yes but, no but" exercise on key questions.

For example, considering the "get thee to a nunnery" conversation between Hamlet and Ophelia:

➔ Is Hamlet mad?

Yes - If he is genuinely mad, then the scene when he tells Ophelia "get thee to a nunnery" is a tragedy – he's been driven insane through grief, the sense of betrayal from his mother and uncle, and he's destroying his relationship with the one person he seems to have shown genuine love for, considering the letters she has received. It heightens the sense of drama that he has lost control.

No - if he's **not** mad, then it's extremely cruel. He's destroying his relationship, insulting and hurting Ophelia for reasons beyond her control and his treatment of her, including his rejection, ultimately lead to her death.

➜ Does he know he's being watched?

Yes – he's deliberately goading Ophelia and the watchers because he knows that she's doing what she's been told by her father, and so he's feeling hurt and rejected himself: she's listened to Polonius and failed to trust Hamlet. He wants the watchers to think he's mad to lull them into false security so they'll reveal their part in his father's death.

No – he's either mad (see above) or Laertes and Polonius are right and he's been toying with Ophelia's affections all along, and is now rejecting her. He's hurt by his mother's remarriage, and is taking out his emotional pain on Ophelia, blaming all women for his mother's apparent wrongs.

HOW TO FORM PRACTICE QUESTIONS: AS LEVEL

There is a very specific format to these questiosn:

"Statement". How far and in what ways do you agree with the given view?

To create practice questions, mind-map a list of themes and characters. Then for each one – working in a group is best for this! – create a slightly controversial statement. You'll need something to argue about! You can also use critics' views as the statement if you come across particularly interesting ones.

There's some examples below of the kind of statements that I use for practice, always with the added "how far and in what ways…" tagged onto the end.

CHARACTER-BASED QUESTIONS
- As the play unfolds it becomes increasingly difficult to sympathize with Hamlet.
- Hamlet (or replace with another character, e.g. Horatio) stands out as a good character in a dark, corrupt world
- At crucial moments, Hamlet's cowardice is what holds him back.
- In the end, the audience can sympathize with none of the main characters.
- A great surprise of the play is that Claudius has a conscience
- It is the discovery of his mother's shallowness and sensuality that is the key to Hamlet's attitude, not the murder of his father.
- Gertrude is a woman more powerful than her time allows.
- The minor characters in Hamlet hold more attraction to the audience than the main protagonists.
- "Frailty, thy name is woman." How appropriate do you find Hamlet's exclamation when you consider the roles of Ophelia and Gertrude in the play?
- The women in Hamlet are little more than plot devices for the male protagonists' conflict.
- Ophelia is simply a lens through which to view the patriarchal world of the play.
- Hamlet's madness is a distraction, for both characters and the audience
- Gertrude is a woman torn between husband and son, and unable to make a choice.

THEME-BASED QUESTIONS:

- Hamlet is a play in which actions speak louder than words.
- A play about self-discovery.
- A play driven by disguise and deception.
- *Hamlet* is a play more about internal than external conflict
- Despite its tragic outcome, *Hamlet* often conveys humour and warmth.
- Political success, power and status often seems very unattractive.
- Nobody truly loves in *Hamlet*.
- The core of the play is the conflict between good and evil.
- The central theme of *Hamlet* is his inability to come to terms with reality
- Reason is more important in the play than passion.
- The desire for justice is an overwhelming concern in *Hamlet*.
- "'Seems', madam? I know not 'seems'" At its heart, *Hamlet* is a play about acting and pretense.

FORM AND STRUCTURE

ELIZABETHAN TRAGEDY

- The ending is catastrophic, often including the death of the main character
- The ending's tragedy is caused by an inherent flaw in the protagonist
- The hero has something interesting or compelling in him anyway, which means we care about his misfortune

This stems from Aristotle's *Poetics* which defines tragedy and comedy. He also said that tragedy, as a genre, acts as a **catharsis** – the audience is emotionally purged and soothed by experiencing these heightened emotions, including the final, often violent, end.

How to apply this:

The genre conventions mean we as an audience have an expectation of what will happen – it's almost more about waiting to see *how* it all happens. At key moments, the tragic nature of the play means we think we know what Hamlet will do – he has to pause in the Chapel scene, for example, because it's too early, structurally, for his crucial battle with Claudius. Hamlet's downfall is inevitable.

We can also discuss *what* his flaw is. Is it madness, the inability to reason and therefore forgive? Is it his filial duty to his father, prompting him to commit multiple murders himself?

REVENGE TRAGEDY

This genre was begun by Thomas Kyd in his *Spanish tragedy* (1587), which was incredibly popular. Most revenge tragedies include some common elements:

- A wronged ghost encouraging revenge on its behalf
- Gory, violent vengeance
- A protagonist with a grievance against an opponent
- A convoluted *private* solution – appeals to public justice are no good
- A tragic ending – often a bloodbath

The Duchess of Malfi (on the OCR A-Level specification) is also a revenge tragedy.

How to apply this:

The revenge tragedy sets up several key expectations. The appearance of the ghost very early on tells an audience familiar with this format what they will see unfold in front of them. The violence of the vengeance also suggests an eventual final set-piece, impressive on stage, rather than the quiet secret murder that could have taken place in the chapel scene. Vengeance has to be over the top, explosive and unequivocal. It also positions Hamlet in some ways as the wronged hero seeking justice in a world he knows will deny it to him – giving him no choice but to seek it for himself. However, as with all this genre, there is a question for the audience of moral judgement: is it justice Hamlet seeks or vengeance? Can he be described at any point as *heroic*?

The Five Act Structure

Hamlet follows a fairly typical five-act structure: exposition, rising action, climax, falling action and denouement. In Act One, we meet the characters and the conflict is established, the emotional climax comes in Act Three when Hamlet's madness appears to grow, he confronts Ophelia and then fails to kill Claudius. The resolution of Act Five comes in just two scenes (albeit one relatively long in the text but, as a fight, can be quite pacy).

How to apply this:

This is a typical convention, and Renaissance playwrights frequently used this structure – audiences knew what they were getting. Many modern plays, books and films use this structure too, changing the relative length of each section. It's a relatively chronological structure, and in Hamlet, quite evenly spaced – from the Act 3 scene 3 moment of Hamlet's indecision, we move onto a falling action until the end. From that perspective, the structure directs us to believe that the play is *all* about Hamlet's choice over whether or not to kill Claudius.

META-THEATRE

"Meta theatre" means a play drawing attention to the theatricality of itself, and there's a few different instances of this in Shakespeare, and particularly in *Hamlet*. The ghost's references to being 'below' with the knowledge of the trap-door beneath the stage, for example, draws attention to its lack of realism but asks the audience to knowingly suspend disbelief.

Ironically, the use of the "play within a play" also draws attention to the theatricality of the **rest** of the play in some respects. It serves two seemingly conflicting purposes – it makes the rest of the play more real, because the other play is fiction. It also heightens some of the fictitious elements of *Hamlet* and reminds us that much of what is going on with the characters is also performative – Hamlet performs elements of madness to confuse the other characters, Claudius uses pomp and ceremony to mask his underhanded deeds. Hamlet instructs the lead player on his speech and how to deliver it, suggesting that Hamlet himself has a very good understanding indeed of how to be an actor.

> *For an excellent discussion of meta-theatre in Hamlet and A Midsummer Night's Dream, see:*
> https://marnielangeroodiblog.wordpress.com/201
> 3/06/05/metadrama-in-two-of-shakespeares-best-
> known-plays-Hamlet-and-a-midsummer-nights-
> dream/

How to apply this:

In *Hamlet,* Shakespeare acknowledges, even celebrates, the theatre and the theatrical. By drawing attention to it he both encourages his audience to enjoy it and he encourages them to accept it. He also considers the fact that life, in many ways, is a performance as well. Macbeth's famous line "all the world's a stage" should resonate for modern audiences, particularly those who are frequently viewing others' highlights on social media, and in *Hamlet* Shakespeare draws attention to the ways that these characters perform themselves, and put on a mask before the rest of the world around them.

EXPLORING SCENE AND ACT TRANSITIONS

When it comes to structure, it's often very useful to look at the changes in scene, and what these can represent. For example, there are frequently rhyming couplets at the end of the scenes – which, as I've noted in the analysis above, often summarise the action thus far and propel us forward to future events.

How to apply this:

1. **Consider scene location**. The **vast** majority of the scenes are "a room in the castle" so when there's a change, consider it significant. The platform and the graveyard, for example, where the ghost is seen are liminal spaces on the edge of the castle and its exterior, and the graveyard having the inherent connection with death perhaps also functioning as a warning to Hamlet of the ghost's true disruptive nature.
2. **Scene and act endings,** Towards the beginning of the play the rhyming couplets are predominately Hamlet speaking, but as the play

continues Claudius gets more of the ending couplets. Is this perhaps suggestive of a further shift in power? After all, Claudius is the one who directs the action in the second half of the play and creates the plot leading to the final duel.

3. **The ending** – Fortinbras finishes the play. Shakespeare resolves the disruption caused by the Hamlet/Claudius feud, and ends with a noble, honourable king taking control of the country.

TIMING

The timeline of the play's unclear – Hamlet refers in 1.1 to it being "two months" since his father's death, and immediately after his mother's marriage. Yet he's unaware of Horatio's presence, who claims to have come for the funeral – although it's possible that Hamlet's response that in fact he came for the wedding is perhaps a dig at his lateness? Hamlet also exaggerates the speed of the marriage to criticise it further.

How to apply this:

Hamlet's madness progress quickly and the question over the speed at the beginning of the play could be Hamlet criticising his mother further, or a genuine length of time. Within the play itself, another two-four months passes between Hamlet seeing the ghost and his "mad" wanderings around the castle, meaning his change in behaviour is relatively fast – does this cast doubt on the genuine nature of his madness, or confirm it?

HOW TO USE FORM AND STRUCTURE TO GET AO2 MARKS

Let's be honest – a closed book exam can be very intimidating.
Especially with a text like *Hamlet*, it can be overwhelming – where do you start to learn what you need?

As with the rest of this guide, there's no substitute for knowing the text and this is a tool to help you – but you don't have to learn all Hamlet's soliloquies or become a Shakespearean scholar to do well.

"Form, structure and language" is usually the most intimidating aspect but it **doesn't** have to involve learning reams of quotations.

The questions are asking for **quotation and references** – which means that a mixture is a brilliant idea. There's also a line from Alan Bennett's *The History Boys* which sums this up:

> *"Remember boys: festoon your answers with gobbets, and you won't go far wrong."*

This suggests a scattershot of quotation, and can be incredibly useful. When revising, recall words used to describe a character – Ophelia, for example, is "fair", "pale", "celestial",. "beautified", "nymph". A handful of words – but together they portray Ophelia as beautiful but weak, the passive female unable to act other than as commanded by others.

Take this example:

> *The play opens with Bernardo's 'Who's there?' and this abrupt interrogative immediately creates an atmosphere of uncertainty and mistrust,*

In the OCR example answer, this is credited with 'close textual detail', but it's hardly memorising the whole of to be or not to be! It's a very simple quote: it's the point of it being **abrupt** and **at the opening of the** play which is important – structure. There's also this:

> *Hamlet's soliloquies become increasingly tormented as he argues with himself, and the actions he believes he must take as a result of the ghost's instructions. As Hamlet progressively appears to become madder, his physical appearance onstage often changes markedly as well*

The idea of **dramatic effect** is also worth thinking about. This goes nicely with "different interpretations" (AO5) which can be linked to the critical interpretations (explored in an earlier section) but also is about the way the audience responds. So:

> *Ophelia's song highlights her madness. Riddled with sexual imagery and innuendo that a girl of her status shouldn't be aware of, the use of the music also makes her seem almost eerily ethereal. It also contrasts with Hamlet's 'mad' language which tends to be prose – the language often used in Shakespeare to denote the lower status characters – which supports the argument that his madness is indeed feigned.*

Again, not a lot of quotation here, but very specific reference – the songs – and an explanation which clearly shows an audience's response. The use of contrast also brings in a structural element, considering characters as foils for one another.

So, how do we work this into revision?

Focus more on structure and the text as a whole.

For example, when revising the role of Claudius, instead of turning to his first speech to the court, brainstorm what is memorable about it – where was it, when was it, why was it delivered that way, what does it look like onstage, why is it important to the rest of the play.

- Regal
- His use of the royal "We" - signals his authority
- Measured and stately, blank verse throughout
- The first time he's addressing the court – the need to assert himself and ensure they are on his side
- Introducing his new wife – a pivotal moment when he needs the court's trust.
- Stagecraft – they all enter together but then what? Are Claudius and Gertrude together? Is Hamlet beside them or skulking at the back? What does that imply? Where were they in different versions – on thrones, or in the centre of the court?
- The contradictions in his language ("With mirth in funeral and with dirge in marriage") which suggest that all is not as comfortable as he's trying to make it sound

There's just the one quote – and you could probably get away without that, too, by referring to the contradiction. But expanding on this detail and exploring its implications, here in note form, you'd have a very solid analysis of FSL without having to remember quotes.

Personally, I'd always find that easier to remember than worrying about getting quotes exactly right. As Matilda in Mister Pip would say: "it's gist." Only, in this case, used in a precise and analytical way.

CHOOSING KEY QUOTATIONS TO REMEMBER

So, although you can use form and structure to get AO2 marks, you do need to know some quotes to show your knowledge of the text. Here's some ways to find them:

- Read past essays – if you've used the quote regularly, then it's probably important! Combine your quotes with others in your class.
- Identify the key quote from each scene

- Identify the quote that, for you, shows you the truth of each major character
- Make a mind-map of words and very short quotes about each character or theme

TOP QUOTATIONS:

Here's my top fifteen – I couldn't narrow it to ten! - in no particular order – but yours could – and probably should! – be different:

Frailty, thy name is woman. (Hamlet's soliloquy after Claudius has announced the marriage, I, i)

I shall obey you (Ophelia to Polonius, I,iii, and Gertrude to Claudius, III, i)

That one may smile and smile and be a villain (Hamlet, on Claudius, I, v)

With mirth in funeral and with dirge in marriage (Claudius announcing the marriage, I, ii)

My crown, mine own ambition and my queen (Claudius, not willing to give up what he's won, III, iii)

Almost as bad good mother
as kill a king and marry with his brother. (Hamlet to Gertrude, III, iv)

Revenge his most foul and unnatural murder (Ghost, I, v)

…foul deeds will rise,
Though all the earth o'erwhelm them, to men's eyes. (Hamlet, I, ii)

My soul is full of discord and dismay (Claudius iv, i)

Each toy seems prologue to some great amiss (Gertrude, IV, v)

'tis an unweeded garden,
That grows to seed; things rank and gross in nature (Hamlet, I, ii)

I doubt it is no other but the main;
His father's death, and our o'erhasty marriage. (Gertrude, II, ii)

'Doubt thou the stars are fire;
Doubt that the sun doth move;
Doubt truth to be a liar;
But never doubt I love (Hamlet, II, ii)

Tender yourself more dearly (Polonius to Ophelia I, iii)

She's so conjunctive to my life and soul,
That, as the star moves not but in his sphere,
I could not but by her (Claudius, IV, vi)

GLOSSARY OF LITERARY TERMS-COMPLETE

Literary vocabulary is assessed as part of AO1 and AO2 but the most important thing, above all else, is to be able to fully interpret the play's themes and ideas. The vocabulary is helpful because it can make your writing more concise and academic – but you must explore your ideas and interpretations using it, rather than simply feature-spotting.

The divides between form, structure and language are also included primarily to make sure that you cover elements of all three in your answer, supporting you in meeting all the assessment objectives.

FORM

*Form: what makes this a **play**? The type or style of a text*

Blank verse	Unrhymed iambic pentameter – often used to lend formality to a speech
Poetry	Rhymed and rhythmic speech – usually using iambic pentameter – often used to heighten the drama and formality of a speech further.
Prose	Unrhymed, unrhythmic speech – as you would get in a novel – often used for a lower-class character *or* to represent the intimacy of a relationship
Revenge tragedy	A genre type, usually beginning with a ghost seeking vengeance for something done to them. The play includes violent, gory scenes, a private seeking of revenge, and a bloodbath at the end.
Stage directions	The instructions from a writer to an actor/director – in Shakespeare's work there are very few (because he was usually writing for a company he was working very closely with, and not for publication unlike playwrights today) – so those that *are* there are particularly important
Proxemics	The movement and placement of characters onstage

STRUCTURE

*Structure: the **organization and narrative shape** of a play.*

Act / scene	The sections / divisions of a play – the equivalent of a novel's chapters, perhaps.
Anaphora	Repeating the beginning of phrases
Antithesis	A person or idea that is the direct opposite of something else.
Collocation	Two or more words that occur together in the same order more than usually would occur, e.g. "fish and chips".
Foil	One character providing a contrast or comparison with another e.g. Hamlet and Laertes' attitudes to their fathers and honour
Hyperbaton	A change in the expected grammatical structure e.g. Some rise by sin, and some by virtue fall
Iambic pentameter	Five sets of 2 iamb (unstressed/stressed syllable pattern) per line - da DUM da DUM da DUM da DUM da DUM
Repetition	A repeated phrase, word or image for effect
Rhyme	Two or more words sounding the same
Rhyming couplet	A set of two lines that rhyme, often at the end of a speech, to give a sense of finality. Frequently sums up the main point/emotion of the speech
Rhythm	The pattern of stressed/unstressed syllables in a line
Soliloquy	A speech spoken by a character to themselves or the audience, usually revealing their thought process
Sub-plot	Another plot strand which is not the main plot
Syndetic	Using conjunctions (and, because) to connect several clauses in a row
Syntax	The order in which the words are written.

LANGUAGE

The vocabulary choices made by a writer

Alliteration	Words close together beginning with the same letter or sound
Allusion	A reference to another story or idea e.g. the Bible
Archaism	An old-fashioned phrase for the time
Assonance	Repeated vowel sounds
Euphemism	A kind or pleasant way of saying something unpleasant
Metaphor	Describing one thing as being something else
Personification	Giving inanimate objects/things human characteristics
Pronoun	Referring to a person or thing e.g. you, me, this
Sibilance	Repeated "s" or "f" sounds
Simile	Comparing one thing to another using like or as
Symbol	A representation of something else.

EXAMPLE ESSAY

"HAMLET IS A PLAY MORE ABOUT INTERNAL THAN EXTERNAL CONFLICT". HOW FAR AND IN WHAT WAYS DO YOU AGREE WITH THIS VIEW? (30 MARKS)

Although *Hamlet's* internal conflict – the potential deterioration of Hamlet's sanity, his indecision over whether to act against Claudius – is often provoked by external conflict – the death of Claudius, and his "o'erhasty" marriage to Gertrude – the internal struggle of Hamlet himself has, over time, become more and more the essential conflict of the play, epitomized in the immortal line "to be, or not to be". Whether debating the role of passion versus reason in Hamlet's inaction, or quoting select, popularized lines ("there are more things in heaven and earth, Horatio"), it is the internal conflict, rather than the feuding or indeed the external political drama, which has made Hamlet ever more popular.

The internal conflict is certainly provoked by external conflict, the "foul and most unnatural murder" of King Hamlet by his brother. Beginning the play mid-conversation ("who's there>") creates an immediate sense of a place unsettled, the audience entering into something they don't understand. A ghost is the conventional beginning to the revenge tragedy but also symbolizes the external conflicts of the world in which Denmark currently exists, something is "rotten" and must be solved before the country – and the rulers of it – can be peaceful.; Even in Claudius' initial speech, the internal and external conflicts are clear: his announcement of his marriage to Gertrude is measured, stately and poetic in blank verse but riddled with internal contradictions: "With mirth in funeral, and with dirth in marriage". Though he might try, Claudius can't mask the internal conflict of his increasing difficulty, which comes to a climax in the chapel scene where he feels unable to pray and ask for forgiveness, because he does not feel guilt as he should and is unwilling to give up "my crown, mine own ambition, and my queen." Although arguably Claudius' conflict becomes externalized in his own plots against Hamlet, first to remove him to England to be murdered and then conspiring with Laertes, he is attempting to resolve his own internal conflict: his desire to get away with murder and enjoy its spoils without the punishment he knows he should expect.

While for Claudius, internal conflict provokes external resolution, the external conflicts experienced by Hamlet manifest themselves in internal conflict. His initial soliloquy expresses his conflict between obeying what he knows to be God's law, and his own desire to end his life; "that the Everlasting had not fix'd His canon 'gainst self-slaughter". Hamlet's soliloquies become increasingly

99

tormented as he argues with himself, and the actions he believes he must take as a result of the ghost's instructions. As Hamlet progressively appears to become more mad, his physical appearance onstage often changes markedly as well. Although Hamlet's madness is questioned – he frequently speaks prose when 'mad' – and it suits him – yet retains his intellectual ability to play with words and perform linguistic gymnastics with both Gertrude and Claudius.

Further external conflicts in the play have been diminished over time, for example the political conflicts between Norway and Denmark, often reducing Fortinbras' role even to the point of removing him completely (Zeffirelli, Olivier) and giving his final lines and role to Horatio. In contrast, the inner conflict of Hamlet's decision-making has become the heart of the play. Hamlet's initial conflict is the misery over his father's death, an "unmanly grief" according to Claudius, and even his mother asks him to put aside his mourning clothes. Yet as the ghost reveals its murder, Hamlet's conflict increase exponentially; does he kill Claudius and avenge his father? Should he disobey his father's command to leave Gertrude to her conscience? Hamlet's indecision has provoked critics to comment on his overly rationalized thought process in the chapel scene, with Johnson arguing that his desire to send Claudius to hell made the scene "too terrible to utter", while Romantics including Coleridge see Hamlet as paralyzed by the strength of his emotions. Yet the latter problem of Gertrude seems to provide most of Hamlet's internal conflict, coming to terms not only with his mother's re-marriage but her potential complicity in his father's death and her sexuality. Whether this is, as Freud suggested, a result of Hamlet's Oedipus complex or instead an Elizabethan disquiet over an older woman's apparent sexual appetite ("You cannot call it love; for at your age / The hey-day in the blood is tame"). Again, while the internal conflict becomes externalized in Hamlet's vicious attack on Gertrude – including his sexual imagery tinged with disgust ("rank sweat of an enseamed bed") and sometimes portrayed with physical violence – it is Hamlet's inner conflict which drives the scene.

Ultimately, although the conflicts in 'Hamlet' are myriad, and will no doubt further shift in interest as Shakespearean scholarship continues, it is C.S. Lewis who encapsulates the question of whether internal, or external, conflict is the prevailing force. In 'Hamlet', "the real and lasting mystery of our human situation has been greatly depicted" – 'Hamlet' endures because in it, Shakespeare explores the mysteries of grief and loss, love and jealousy, madness and sanity – qualities which all humanity may experience, may even recognize externally, but which we must all struggle with within ourselves.

ABOUT THE AUTHOR

Learning about literature. For smart people.

I have written a series of revision guides for A-Level, available at my website – www.charlotteunsworth.com – and on Amazon: https://www.amazon.co.uk/-/e/B00BCP1HC2

I love stories - reading them, writing them, exploring them. Delving in, so that it becomes a part of me and the way I understand the world. I teach English at Skipton Girls' High School, North Yorkshire, sharing my enthusiasm for literature and belief in its importance in our society. I blog regularly at http://www.charlotteunsworth.com on literature and teaching.

I write regularly, trying to write something every day. I have published stories in several anthologies, and literary criticism in journals including The Uses of English, and E-Magazine.

Follow me on twitter (@miss_tiggr).

25067475R00060

Printed in Great Britain
by Amazon